Negotiating the Maze of School Reform

*How Metaphor Shapes Culture
in a New Magnet School*

Jean Wincek

Foreword by Bernice McCarthy

Teachers College, Columbia University
New York and London

Published by Teachers College Press, 1234 Amsterdam Avenue, New York, NY 10027

Library of Congress Cataloging-in-Publication Data

Wincek, Jean, 1939–
    Negotiating the maze of school reform : how metaphor shapes
culture in a new magnet school / Jean Wincek.
        p.   cm.
    Includes bibliographical references and index.
    ISBN 0-8077-3413-6 (cloth : acid-free paper).–ISBN
0-8077-3412-8 (paper : acid-free paper)
    1. Magnet schools–United States–Case studies.   2. Educational
change–United States–Case studies.   3. Educational innovations–
United States–Case studies.   I. Title.
LB2818.W56   1995
370'.01–dc20   94-42645

ISBN 0-8077-3412-8 (paper)
ISBN 0-8077-3413-6 (cloth)
Printed on acid-free paper
Manufactured in the United States of America
02 01 00 99 98 97 96 95   8 7 6 5 4 3 2 1

To the CSJ's
who have nurtured my love of learning
since kindergarten
and
In memory of my parents,
Walter and Bernice Wincek

Contents

Foreword

This book is a chronicle of the first year of Mega Center, a magnet school in a large, midwestern, urban district. It is about a courageous group of educators who undertook a vision of reform—a vision of how children learn, how teaching should be conducted, and how leadership could work. It tells of their joys and their conflicts, their accomplishments and their failings. It speaks of the complex and tangled threads comprising the education enterprise—an enterprise so intricate and interconnected that the whole never entirely appears. Jean Wincek takes us through the emerging culture and into the development of school-wide metaphorical language, language that is crucial to the success of the shared vision.

There are many books that chronicle the intricacies of educational reform. Most illuminate the pitfalls of innovation in clear detail. Most leave us with few solutions and little hope.

This book is different. This book suggests a path through the maze. The author believes that the examination of the metaphors embedded in people's beliefs about who they are and what they do is critical for the establishment of a shared vision. She contends that metaphors form the heart of the conceptualizations people have about what things mean and how things work. She believes that if leadership can tap into these understandings and bring them forth—where they can be examined, enjoyed, and challenged—the task of reform can begin. A bridge can be built between vision and practice.

I know a little bit about how difficult real change is. I have witnessed teams of teachers excited, moved, and enthusiastic about an innovation. I have watched as they participated in really fine, professional training. I have returned a month later only to find little or nothing changed.

If I am sure of anything in my professional experience it is that implementation is messy stuff. It moves in starts and fits. Worthy innovations take teacher time. The author shows us how, on numerous occasions, sufficient time was not taken to probe assumptions, to create operational reflective learning environments where people could clarify meanings.

Yet for an innovation to flourish, teachers need both to act and to reflect in a kind of rhythm, to practice, to watch practice, to receive feedback and to give feedback, to be thoughtful with each other about teaching.

This atmosphere of trust takes a special kind of listening, a way of being Carl Rogers terms empathic: "moving about delicately, without judgement, laying aside the views and values one holds in order to enter the other's world without prejudice. A complex, demanding, strong yet subtle and gentle way of being."

This kind of teacher time (time away from students) is simply not available in schools. And teachers receive little training in the necessary interpersonal skills described here for the kind of sharing needed to accomplish real change.

As the culture of Mega Center emerged in that first key year, it became apparent that there were differences in teachers beliefs and meanings regarding the reform. But the teaching and learning enterprise had to go on. The children were there. The teaching tasks could not wait. The teachers were modifying their teaching practices, changing roles, altering relationships, and doing an outstanding job of teaching children, all at the same time. They were no longer teaching alone with one class, no longer just giving information, no longer teaching subjects in isolation. They needed time and a climate safe and open to experimentation, where they could make mistakes and discuss what they were learning from those mistakes.

Many of us have been there, have engaged in innovation that we believed was worthy and well received only to be disappointed in the results. This book presents us with a promising practice. If people can become skilled in the use of metaphors to describe the meanings they attribute to their beliefs, their lives, and their work, and if climates of trust can be called into existence to permit a sharing of those metaphors, then the dialogue can begin in earnest. The author concludes that unless reflective examination of personal and institutional metaphors occurs, transformation will not take place. The process of real growth is directly dependent upon such clarity of vision.

So the reader is taken through this first exciting and difficult year in a magnet school. The clashes, the disparities in belief and meaning, and the instances where time was not taken and should have been, because it would have made a difference, are all pointed out and illuminated. We see the lost opportunities.

But we also see poignant meaning in this chronicle. We feel the triumphs, the belief in the unique worthiness of each child, the school-wide pride, the successes with the children that abound throughout the book. We realize anew how necessary and worthwhile educational reform is and how courageous those who undertake such reform really are.

Bernice McCarthy
President, Excel, Inc.

Preface

Mega Center for Learning is a pseudonym for a magnet school established in 1990 in a large midwestern urban school district. Its beginnings go back to the early 1980s when a school board member began planting seeds of interest in the minds of other board members, the district office staff, and community members. She wondered, in part, how the principles and practices used successfully in gifted education might be applied in regular classroom settings. In 1989 the seeds germinated when the district received a grant to create a school that incorporated the findings of research on how children learn best with practical arrangements that would support creative ways of teaching and learning.

The newly hired district staff development director took the lead in planning Mega Center's program. Initially he had envisioned having a yearlong series of workshops for teachers in the district who might be interested in teaching at Mega Center. The workshops would have included topics such as cross-age grouping of children, family involvement in schools, styles of learning, inclusion of all children in regular classrooms, and Howard Gardner's theory of multiple intelligences. According to his plan, district teachers who participated in the workshops and who expressed interest in teaching at Mega Center would have constituted the pool of applicants for the new faculty. The plan called for Mega Center to open as a K–3 program in the 1991–1992 school year.

In the meantime, space was becoming a critical issue for the district. Older neighborhood schools were having problems meeting fire codes and finding ground-floor space for the burgeoning number of primary-age students. State monies became available for acquiring buildings appropriate for young children, and the district had to move quickly to capitalize on this opportunity.

The district procured a new building in the fall of 1989. At first district officials proposed using the building as a kindergarten and first-grade center for the children from all surrounding neighborhood schools. At public hearings on the issue, parents vigorously protested this plan. They wanted the building to house a magnet program. The school board relented and in April 1990 voted to initiate and fund the Mega Center for Learning program in the building for 240 K–3 students beginning in the 1990–1991 school year, a full year earlier than program planners anticipated.

Early in May, after a week of interviewing, the superintendent appointed a principal for Mega Center. After the new principal and the district staff development director conducted informational sessions for parents of prospective students, parents applied for the school of their choice. By the first week of June, the district had received over 400 applications for the new program. Because of the high interest, the superintendent decided to increase the student enrollment from 240 to 400.

District officials and the new principal began interviewing teachers for Mega Center during the second week in June. "We wanted teachers who would match curriculum to kids, not vice versa," commented the new principal. Hired by the last week in June, teachers began an abbreviated version of the projected yearlong training. Staff development sessions occurred in segments of two weeks on, two weeks off throughout the summer. During their weeks off teachers reported that they were busy moving from their former schools, doing reading on topics suggested in workshops, and planning curriculum for their new school.

And so begins the story of Mega Center. Resulting from a yearlong study, this book chronicles the school's first year, focusing on how the primary metaphors embedded in the school's descriptive documents and in the minds and practices of Mega Center's stakeholders helped or hindered efforts at educational reform. The book records both the successes of educators committed to helping children strive for excellence and the conflict, stress, and ambiguity resulting from an unarticulated diversity of understandings regarding key operational metaphors.

The first chapter sets the stage for the study while the second lays out the research plan. Chapter 3 surveys the history of schooling in the United States since the late 1800s, emphasizing metaphors included in major movements. This history forms the context out of which the district and Mega Center planners drew their impetus for change. Chapter 4 examines the power of metaphor, looks at what researchers are suggesting as changing roles and relationships in schools, and links these two ideas to the notion of school culture. Chapters 5 through 8 address Mega Center's four major institutional meta-phors—vision, families, teams, and vision-keeper—showing the influ-ence of these metaphors on changing educational practices and on shaping the school's culture. Chapter 9 focuses on making connec-tions between the major metaphors operative during Mega Center's start-up year and the diverse images of schooling found in the history of school reform and in educational literature on improving schools. Also this chapter proposes ways Mega Center and other schools en-gaged in reform efforts can begin to forge stronger links between their language and their practice.

Although this book tells the story of a new magnet school, every school concerned about addressing the needs of students will do well to heed its message. Educators must ask themselves who is being served by prevailing structures, roles, and relationships. Uncovering the metaphors that reflect beliefs and undergird practice can provide a basis for reforming school cultures and creating new American schools.

Acknowledgments

At times, doing research and writing a book can be a mazelike experience. However, many supportive and generous people have influenced me and helped me see my way more clearly. To each and every one I owe my appreciation.

Because I use pseudonyms throughout the book, I cannot personally name those closest to Mega Center's heartbeat, but I want to thank them using their pseudonyms. My thanks go to school board member Frances Meyer and to school district staff development director Paul Elson for rearranging busy schedules to accommodate my interviews. I owe a tremendous debt of gratitude to the students, teachers, staff, and parents at Mega Center for opening their school and their lives to me during their first year together. Special thanks to the teachers for their trust, their honesty, and their time, a precious resource in the lives of educators. I extend deep gratitude to school principal Suzanne Dawson, who opened Mega Center's doors to me from the very first day, giving me access to the peaks and valleys of the school's first year. I am grateful for her hospitality, for her candor, and for her support.

My gratitude goes also to my friends and readers at the University of St. Thomas—Steven Preskill, Tullio Maranhão, Hallie Preskill, and Karen Rogers—four women and men whose ideas challenged my thinking, whose expertise gave me insight, whose experience provided me with new resources, and whose support sustained my efforts. I also thank Katherine Egan, Thomas McCarver, and Karen Ristau from St. Thomas for their encouragement throughout this process.

I am deeply grateful for the generosity of my friend and editor, Judith Faulkner McGuire. Her critique of each chapter pushed me to clarify my thought, to keep my focus, and to sharpen my writing. Combining personal support, reflective conversation, and technical skill, she gave me momentum and reassurance as I moved from outline through multiple drafts to final copy.

While working on this project I sometimes asked myself, "Why am I doing this?" The next ring of the telephone was likely to bring an answer. I am grateful to my sister, Mary Lou Rainville, for sharing with me her insights into educational issues as she and her husband, Edward, faced large and small questions on schooling for their three sons, Jeremy, Joel, and Jay. In our conversations I heard the voice of a parent with visions of what excellent education is or could be for her children. She assured me that examining the issue of school reform was a worthwhile study.

Throughout my years in the educational field I have been privileged to meet and to work with outstanding teachers and staff members, too numerous to name here. There are, however, seven friends and educators whose love of children inspires me and whose dreams and ideals challenge me. To Maureen Greenberg, Jane McDonald, Amy McManus, Marianne Mortenson, Tim Subialka, Diane Wielinski, and my colleague Colleen O'Malley, I say thank you for your constancy and your wisdom. A special word of thanks to Colleen, who assisted me in conducting children's and parents' focus-group interviews, who listened and shared insights as my ideas took shape, who read and critiqued portions of the manuscript, and who encouraged me when the project felt overwhelming.

Thanks, too, to Jill Reilly, who reviewed an early version of the manuscript, and to Judith Kavanaugh, who tracked down an account of the adventures of Theseus for me after I told her the story of Jason's maze from the first chapter.

Finally, a thank you to Susan Liddicoat and Peter Sieger at Teachers College Press for thoughtfully guiding me and my work through the review, editing, and production processes. I am grateful for their counsel and their direction.

Negotiating the Maze of School Reform

How Metaphor Shapes Culture in a New Magnet School

Theseus did exactly as he was told, and next day entered the Labyrinth with the clue of thread concealed in his hand. When alone, he attached one end to the lintel of the door, and unwound the thread behind him as he traced his way through the winding passages, leading up and down, hither and thither, until he came to the great chamber or cavern in the center where dim light from above showed the monster waiting for him. [He destroyed the monster,] and after resting a little, Theseus picked up the end of the thread, and began to follow it back, winding it up as he went. . . . In time he grew weary of his peaceful life, and longed for further adventures. So he was overjoyed when a message reached him from a young prince called Jason urging him to join in an expedition in search of the Golden Fleece.

–The Adventures of Theseus
Heroes of Greece and Troy
(Retold from the Ancient Authors
by Roger Lancelyn Green)

CHAPTER ONE

The Maze
of School Reform

It was mid-afternoon on the last day of the school year at Mega Center for Learning. Leaving the bright, June sunlight, I opened the heavy, gray metal doors leading from the parking lot to the garden level and climbed the wide terrazzo stairs to the first floor. I had used this stairway hundreds of times during my year of research at Mega Center, but today, the last day of Mega Center's first year of operation, I recalled stair stories I had noted carefully on my yellow legal pad throughout the year. A person could do a study on what happens on stairways in schools.

One day I met an eight-year-old instructing a five-year-old on the art of carrying large loads of lunch boxes back to their classroom after noon recess. Another day a mother coming to volunteer in her son's classroom patiently waited close by while her toddler negotiated the stairs. "He wants to do it himself," she explained. On Valentine's Day, crushed cookies and fine red sugar crunched underfoot on the stairway. Drops of orange drink dotted the stairs on this last day of school. The day before, two seven-year-olds knelt on the stairs sweeping up straw from the dismantling of Charlotte's Web. Assisting with the cleanup, the maintenance engineer said, "If you had asked, I would have bundled the straw so it wouldn't have made such a mess."

As I opened the door to the first-floor hallway, thoughts about this year crowded into my mind. Any one of these stairway vignettes could be a metaphor for an aspect of Mega Center's program. The school's vision of educational reform included peer tutoring, parent involvement, celebration, and experiential learning. But my research focus was broader than these individual elements of innovation.

I

JASON'S MAZE

Making my way down the wide, well-lighted hallway, I headed for the same place I stood on the first day of school when the children arrived wearing yellow, green, blue, or red visors designating their family of learners. When I was halfway to my destination, Jason, a blond eight-year-old whose red shorts and black T-shirt showed signs of hard play at recess, stopped me. Proudly he held out a piece of 11-by 14-inch drawing paper covered with short, thin, black magic marker lines. "Did you see the maze I made in about an hour?" he asked. Other children gathered around Jason. I asked him to tell me about his maze and show me how it worked. His finger traced a path from start to finish through the maze. "But there are really lots of ways to do it," he added. I watched as Jason explained to the other children how to make a maze and these eager problem solvers delighted in finding new ways through the maze. As more children gathered around Jason, I thanked him for showing me his maze and continued down the hall toward the foyer near the school office.

Suzanne Dawson, the principal of Mega Center, opened the office door. "What does it feel like to have this be the last hour of the last day?" I asked. "Is it June?" Suzanne quipped. Children skipped past us carrying backpacks, lunch boxes, and shopping bags brimming with personal treasures. "Good bye, Dr. Dawson," they sang. "Have a nice summer." Jason was one of the last to leave. He clutched his maze tightly in his hand as he hurried to catch his bus.

"Did you see Jason's maze?" I asked Suzanne. When I recapped the hallway incident for her, she smiled and sighed. "There are really lots of ways to get through the maze," she repeated quietly. "Out of the mouths of babes."

My experience with Jason and his maze kept coming back as I thought about the year. From one perspective the story captures attitudes and actions I saw every day at Mega Center. In the last hour of the last day of the school year, when children usually engage in partying or cleaning, Jason's interest and motivation led him to focus on creating his maze. His teacher not only allowed him to pursue his interest but supplied him with the materials, space, and support to carry out his project.

He was proud of his work to the point of taking it on a show-and-tell excursion outside the classroom. Leaving his classroom was not a problem because Mega Center is organized in families, and everyone looks out for everyone else. Jason felt safe approaching me to show off his work. All adults at Mega Center are educators and resource persons for the learners.

Interacting with this child who was proud of his work was a magic moment. The maze was not a piece of work handed to a teacher to be graded, but the product of a creative process to be explained, self-evaluated, and affirmed. The learning for Jason happened in the making, explaining, and celebrating. The magic of the moment extended to other children, who learned from a peer how to make a maze and who experienced the joy of problem solving their way through the maze. As an educator, the magic for me was seeing in this child's eyes and hearing in his voice the delight of accomplishment. As researcher I recognized in this chance happening the voices of Mega Center's teachers, parents, and administrators as they explained their visions of how learning happens for children.

THE MAZE OF MEGA CENTER'S FIRST YEAR

At another level, Jason's maze tells the story of Mega Center's first year. Suzanne's smile, sigh, and comment when she heard the story of Jason's maze reveals her insight. Surely not Jason and perhaps not even Suzanne realized how apt a metaphor the maze was as a way to describe the one reality in terms of another.

The Oxford English Dictionary (OED) (1989) cites definitions of *maze* beginning in the thirteenth century. The most commonly used definition is "a structure consisting of a network of winding and intercommunicating paths and passages arranged in bewildering complexity so that without guidance it is difficult to find one's way in it" (p. 507). Sometimes maze refers to "a structure in which there is a single path winding in such a manner that the distance from the entrance to the end is enormously greater than it would be in a direct line" (p. 507). Used in a psychological context, a maze is "a device, consisting of a correct path concealed by blind alleys, used to study human and animal intelligence and learning" (p. 507). A last definition, used in the seventeenth and eighteenth centuries, leads to another metaphor: "A winding movement, especially in a dance" (p. 507).

A Complex Network of Passages. In several interviews, Mega Center teachers described their experiences as complex networks of passages. They struggled through a year in which there were no sure pathways, in which they cut the way as they went, in which they were bewildered by the complexity of the effort, and in which they needed guidance and feedback for reassurance.

Another area of bewilderment centered around the role of the principal. Questions about leadership pervaded the year. Suzanne's struggle to conceptualize leadership from new perspectives is a central part of Mega Center's story.

A Long Winding Path. Mega Center teachers expected to work hard, especially during the school's first year, but often felt overwhelmed because the distances between ideas and implementation were enormously greater and more complex than they had imagined.

Some teachers thought that coming to a newly established school would give them opportunities to do things they had always wanted to do with children. Unmindful of the complex, contradictory, and nonrational qualities of social systems, some teachers expressed dismay over the circuitous paths and blind alleys they encountered during the year. They expressed their reactions in words that are also early definitions of maze: disappointment, dissipation, deception, and bewilderment.

A Device to Study Behavior. There is irony in the use of maze as metaphor for Mega Center's first year. Although the principal and teachers ran down numerous blind alleys in the course of discovering how to achieve educational reform, the school's philosophy expressed belief in multiple paths to learning, in multiple human intelligences, and in success for every child. Jason's comment, "There are really lots of ways to do it," reflects Mega Center's understanding of the learning process for the children. One teacher explained her notion of Mega Center as a kind of lab school in which professionals could try out educational ideas, stretch themselves and their students to their creative limits, and always be on the cutting edge. This is quite different from putting subjects through a laboratory maze. Although teachers experienced school as a maze, the students did not.

A Winding Movement. The definition of maze as a winding movement or dance captures other aspects of the first year of Mega Center's operation: the eagerness to participate, the interplay between following and leading, and the exhilaration of creativity. The principal, Suzanne Dawson, used the dance metaphor to describe the abundance of applications received for teaching positions at Mega Center. "More wanted to come than could dance," she explained to a group of visiting teachers.

Teachers talked of their experience with children as constant, creative movement. "I am constantly challenged to be creative," one teacher volunteered. "I am always moving from the time the children arrive until they leave. It's like a constant dance."

The story of Jason's maze gave me the conceptual tools to think about Mega Center's first year from multiple perspectives. In elucidating the metaphor, I touched on issues central to school improvement: the school's mission, its environment and arrangements for learning, the relationships among professionals, and its leadership. In discussing these aspects of Mega Center's efforts to reform education in Chapters 5, 6, 7, and 8, I will concentrate on relationships between the school's metaphors, its developing culture, and its improvement efforts.

THE CALL TO REFORM SCHOOLS

During the 1980s, the call for academic excellence in America's schools echoed from presidential meetings to legislative debates, from gubernatorial platforms to corporate board rooms, from blue-ribbon committee meetings to professional educational association discussions, from school district offices to faculty lounges, from parent and teacher organization agendas to demands of concerned parents. But American students have continued to fall far behind the students from other nations on international achievement tests (Chubb & Moe, 1990). Although the 1980s was a decade of the "greatest and most concentrated surge of educational reform in the nation's history" (Doyle & Hartle, 1985, p. 1), graduates of American schools do not know enough, do not know the right things, and do not know how to learn. Public criticism of the nation's schools abounds.

Harvard educator Sara Lawrence Lightfoot's (1983) perspective on the public's lack of confidence in schools comes from her investigation of good high schools. She attributes the commonly held belief that schools are woefully inadequate in preparing students to meet the demands of the twenty-first century to "the combined impact of the subtle negativisms of social science investigations and the flagrant attacks of muckrakers over the last few decades" (p. 314). She sees the persistent complaints as reflecting

a powerful combination of romanticism, nostalgia and feelings of loss for a simpler time when values were clear, when children were well behaved, when family and school agreed on educational values and priorities, when the themes of honor, respect and loyalty directed human interaction. (p. 314)

Lightfoot concludes that in light of an idealized retrospective view, the current status of schooling in the United States appears to be cataclysmic.

Lightfoot's analysis points to the importance of examining societal and personal beliefs about the values and purposes of schooling. One way to probe these beliefs and values is to look at images or metaphors about schooling prevalent in educational literature.

REFORM METAPHORS

Diverse and sometimes contradictory metaphors on schooling and school improvement dominate the thinking of policymakers, scholars, and practitioners. For example, a common metaphor for school is the factory. The purpose of the factory is to produce a product that satisfies the needs of the public. Just as machines and the entire environment of the factory respond to rational adjustments to improve the product, the metaphor suggests that every facet of schooling is a candidate for planned change.

A second metaphor, farming, gives another picture of schooling. The farmer's work starts with an ancient and stable process of growth and builds around what the sun, climate, seeds, plants, and insects are likely to do. Understanding the process, the farmer can improve production but must contend with forces over which he has little control. This image provides a fundamentally different way of viewing schooling. Its ramifications for improving schools differ considerably from those of the factory metaphor (Cuban, 1993).

In *Schooling for Tomorrow*, Thomas Sergiovanni (1989) uses the metaphors of surfing and pitching balls to describe school improvement. The pitching metaphor envisions schooling as the delivery of teaching (the ball) to a specified target (the strike zone). Monitoring and refining the delivery system increases the chances of hitting the target of improving student achievement.

In contrast to the methodical improvement image of the pitching-balls metaphor, the surfing metaphor describes the dynamic interplay between the surfer and the waves. The surfer's success depends on making immediate, ongoing decisions in response to the patterns of waves as they emerge. As in surfing, school improvement happens when teachers and principals see the need to adjust to changing circumstances, become informed about the dynamics of a good school, apply their understandings to their unique circumstances, then examine why their decisions had favorable or unfavorable outcomes. School improvement calls for an ongoing process of decision making and reflection. Nonetheless, "school improvement experts often favor the pitching metaphor for schooling, because it is easier to deal with" (Sergiovanni, 1989, p. 3).

Metaphors both shape and reflect each person's values and beliefs. Conversely, values and beliefs shape metaphor and influence language and practice. Both national and personal beliefs about schooling and school improvement affect the public's perception of the effectiveness of schools. Those most affected by public perception are school principals, teachers, and ultimately the children. Over the last century most reform initiatives have aimed at changing teacher behavior (Cuban, 1988a). The changes that endured have strengthened traditional structures, legitimated existing practices, and preserved the prevailing metaphors. On the other hand, changes not sharing traditional metaphors have faded from practice.

To be successful, individual school improvement efforts must touch the school's culture, since the culture emerges from the goals and values that form the core of traditions that gradually develop. Culture includes the complex intermingling of an organization's "history, symbols, myths, rituals, visions, rules, atmosphere, guiding metaphors, ideology and typical patterns of communication" (Thompson, 1986, p. 14). Metaphors have the power to bring to life taken-for-granted ideas embedded in a school's culture.

ONE DISTRICT'S RESPONSE TO REFORM

School reform literature suggests that little change has occurred in the basic structures of schooling in the past century (Cuban, 1988a; Tyack, Kirst, & Hansot, 1980). One reason that few significant changes have endured is that implementation efforts sagged. Behind classroom doors teachers decided what to implement and what not to implement. Regulatory interventions designed to control teachers have not been successful. Successful reformers, recognizing the complexity of schools, initiate changes, then carefully tend them over time (Johnson, 1990).

School districts across the country are responding to public out-
cries and legislative demands for school improvement. Their initiatives
are paving the way for change in individual schools. A reform mecha-
nism popular in many districts is the establishment of magnet or
alternative schools.

In September 1990, a large midwestern urban public school district opened a new magnet school, Mega Center for Learning. Mega
Center is an example of one district's initiative in educational change.
Its professed beliefs, values, and educational practices differ from those
in most other schools in the district. Structural changes support Mega
Center's vision and its commitment to lifelong learning and educational
excellence. Within the context of the emerging culture of a new
magnet school, I examined the metaphors of teachers, administrators,
parents, and students at Mega Center. My study reveals how their
metaphors inform educational practice, sustain or stymie improvement efforts, and give meaning to their experiences.

Districts often use a combination of quantitative and qualitative
methods to evaluate new schools and alternative programs. Another
useful way to view what is happening in schools is to probe their
culture and metaphorical language using qualitative research methods. An ethnographic research study examining the culture of a school
through its metaphors in its first year of operation can offer insight
into how metaphors reveal experience, shape change, and illuminate
the path to new educational paradigms.

In *Ideology, Culture and the Process of Schooling*, Henry Giroux
(1981) describes schools as "social sites whose particularity is characterized by an ongoing struggle between hegemonic and counter-
hegemonic forces" (p. 15). Magnet schools emerge in political con-
texts where external and internal expectations for success are high.
Mega Center is a magnet school in every sense. It owes its existence
to the direct demands of parents for new ways of educating their
children. Because it is a new school, both district and parents have a
keen interest in its emerging culture and scrutinize it carefully. There-
fore, a view of Mega Center's culture through the lens of its metaphors
sheds light on the particular struggles of a magnet school.

Reform efforts can respond to the educational needs of children
only when educators critically examine the assumptions shaping their
language and practice. Careful consideration of the results of this study
can give the Mega Center community and other educators an opportunity to reflect on Mega Center's metaphorical language as well as
its practices and beliefs. In the broader cultural context, the study also
illuminates the effects of dissonance between belief and practice on

any institutional enterprise, be it a newly founded institution like Mega Center or an organization with long-standing traditions.

The locus of this qualitative study is Mega Center for Learning as it struggled to respond to reform initiatives, to articulate new metaphors, and to develop an alternative educational paradigm. The study focuses on the importance of metaphor in revealing experience and shaping change within a political context.

CHAPTER TWO

The Research Plan

In over 25 years of experience in education I have seen trends come and go. I remember inspiring speakers who energized teachers with innovative and well-documented ideas on how to improve the teaching and learning processes. Despite initial enthusiasm, the new ideas quickly faded from memory. I observed school administrators directing their faculties to implement new programs after one exposure to the concept. Behind classroom doors teachers conducted business as usual. My experience confirms my belief that unless the persons promoting innovative ideas understand how school improvement happens and relate that knowledge to the school's culture, teachers will view change initiatives as interference or tinkering.

Teachers resist imposed change. Unless they see either greater efficiencies in their work or improved learning for the children, they quickly and quietly abandon the prescribed reform. Commitment to a reform effort grows out of dialogue in which teachers and principals explore the meaning of the change and develop a picture of what the change might look like when it is implemented. The change begins to happen in the conceptual systems of the persons involved. During the implementation process teachers need to participate in ongoing conversation and training. An essential role of administrators is to support and encourage the persons implementing the change as they experiment with new ideas.

A consistent theme running through educational literature on change, leadership, and the role of the principal is the centrality of leadership in initiating and sustaining change (Hall & Hord, 1987). A critical aspect of the leadership role is the day-to-day action the leader takes to support the change process. These research findings supported my experience. I wondered how the intricate blend of a school's culture and the leader's understanding, articulation, and support of its philosophy, mission, and plans for growth promote and sustain improvement of educational practice.

BEGINNING THE STUDY

My experience raised for me the questions in this study. Seren-
dipity led me to my research site. Seldom would a person have the
opportunity to observe at a school in a newly acquired building,
whose entire faculty, staff, and administration were new to the site
and whose program differs considerably from any other program in
the school district. I applied for and obtained permission from the
school district to do research at Mega Center for Learning during its
first year of operation, from August 1990 through June 1991. Initially
I formulated my research question in broad terms: How do the intricate blend of the school's emerging culture and its understanding
and articulation of its ideological stance promote and sustain improvement efforts?

The first challenge I faced was to find a niche at Mega Center for
Learning. The principal, Suzanne Dawson, made my entry into the
school informal and comfortable. On the advice of the chair of the district research committee, I met with Suzanne prior to submitting my
research proposal to the district. She welcomed me warmly, reviewed
my proposal, and assured me of her support and cooperation. She gave
me an open invitation to attend any meetings she called, and she set
up a mailbox where I would receive internal faculty and staff communications. She introduced me as an ethnographic researcher studying
Mega Center's first year of operation and authorized me to go directly
to teachers to arrange classroom observations and interviews.

The Importance of Language

As I began my year of ethnographic research, two additional
strands of thinking engaged my energies and helped focus my research
question. First, in discussions with colleagues on the role of metaphor
as shaper of beliefs and values and source of action, I came to appre-
ciate how metaphor shapes the human conceptual system, how
speech reveals metaphor, and how language and metaphor influence
practice. I began to gain insight and to find words for what I noted at
my research site.

In one of my first visits to Mega Center I heard the principal and
teachers use new language to describe their roles. "I have been a first-
grade teacher for years," Bea explained, "but now I am a primary
teacher." The principal, Suzanne, talked about how hard it is to get
out of the old paradigm. She explained that she does not want teachers classified by grade level, yet this is the only way the district office

computer will process the teachers' pay. She revealed her awareness of the importance of language in describing the roles of teachers. "When you get a title, you begin to build a paradigm," she said. For another teacher, Kathy, the "primary teacher" definition felt awkward. "I have to keep biting my tongue not to say grade one," she admitted. I wondered if these teachers were simply creating a new educational jargon or if their new language and metaphors signaled new beliefs and practices. I began to focus my study on uncovering the metaphors of teachers, administrators, staff, parents, and students at Mega Center for Learning to see what effect, if any, their metaphors had on their educational practices, their improvement efforts, and their understanding of what was happening for them.

The Context of History

A second issue emerged as I reviewed the history and research on school improvement and reform. My sources referred to images of school that have been part of the history of American education. They reminded me that schools do not exist in isolation but are part of complex social and political systems, which influence and shape what happens in schools. I realized that these systems carry their own metaphors, which can support or stifle school reform efforts. Since Mega Center for Learning represents one school district's response to society's call for change, the context of my study needed to be the history of school reform and the metaphors inherent in that history. I limited this review of the history and metaphors of reform to schools in the United States as they have functioned from the late nineteenth through the twentieth century. I will develop these themes and cite these sources in Chapter 3.

The Examination of Culture

The locus of my study is an individual school with a unique culture. In gathering data necessary to describe and analyze the metaphorical language, beliefs, and practices of this magnet school in its start-up year, I used qualitative research methods. Several approaches to qualitative research exist, with differing assumptions underlying each tradition. One tradition, holistic ethnography, is an attempt "to understand the unique configuration of the culture of a bounded group with a minimum of preconceived ideas or theories" (Jacob, 1987, p. 12). Culture is a central and complex concept in the ethnographic research tradition. The ethnographic researcher assumes that each culture is unique, that individuals in a group share cultural meanings with significant regularity, and that culture does not determine behavior but has a substantial influence on behavior (Jacob, 1987). The nature of my research question necessitated my working within an ethnographic research tradition.

My study looks not only at the emerging culture of Mega Center for Learning, but, within that context, at the metaphorical language of the teachers, principal, parents, and students. In his book *Ethnography Step by Step*, David Fetterman (1989) refines the concept of culture by describing it from a cognitive perspective in which the ideas, beliefs, and knowledge of the group are of primary interest to the researcher. According to Fetterman, "a cognitive definition of culture would orient the ethnographer toward linguistic data: daily discourse" (p. 27). During my first day at the research site, I realized that Mega Center was developing a unique metaphorical language. My research interest became more specific, and I decided to concentrate my study on the linguistic aspect of culture.

ETHNOGRAPHIC METHODOLOGY

Although there is not a standard ethnographic research design, each researcher follows certain basic procedures: gathering data through fieldwork, documenting the participant's point of view, recording verbatim statements, and using a wide range of data-collection methods. Participant observation is the methodology most characteristic of ethnographic research. It affords the researcher the opportunity to participate in the culture, to observe behaviors, and to maintain a professional distance. While any outsider may be intrusive, the least distortion in the culture occurs when qualitative researchers approach people with the intention of trying to understand them (Bogdan & Biklen, 1982).

The design of an ethnographic study evolves as the fieldwork progresses "with a cross-fertilization of analysis and observation" (Jacob, 1987, p. 14). Interviews are the ethnographer's most important data-collection technique because they "explain and put into a larger context what the ethnographer sees and experiences" (Fetterman, 1989, p. 47). Both formal and informal interviews can be useful in data collection. An ethnographer may use focus groups "to identify trends and patterns in perceptions" (Krueger, 1988, p. 18). The researcher samples events, times, and people and continues to collect data until no new information emerges.

Data Gathering

My data-gathering techniques included multiple opportunities to cross-check information. I spent an average of four half days per week at Mega Center. The broad nature of my study required me to become familiar with the school building and to make the acquaintance of all personnel. From the moment I entered the building each day, I wrote notes on what I heard and observed. I took alternate routes to the office where I signed in, looking in each classroom as I passed and noting what was happening. I recorded changes in hallway decorations, taking special note of children's work displayed on the walls. Greeting each teacher, parent, aide, child, and visitor, I often stopped to talk informally or to ask a question.

Classroom Observations. Beginning in September, I observed classes in all classrooms and special programs and conducted informal interviews with teachers, office personnel, parents, students, and the administrator. At least one day ahead, I made arrangements for an observation time of approximately two hours with each teacher. When I entered the classroom, I made a diagram of the room arrangements and noted the contents of all displays and bulletin boards. Paying attention to where children sat, I took detailed notes on verbal and nonverbal interactions among children and between children and the teacher. In many cases I used a tape recorder to capture conversations or the content of the lesson. At times I moved around the room watching the children work individually or in groups and listening to their conversation. Sometimes children enlisted my help or asked my opinion. Occasionally I initiated conversation with them. When children worked independently, teachers often offered me unsolicited thoughts about the school.

Informal Conversations. As I came to and went from the office, I had opportunities for spontaneous interviews with parents, office personnel, visitors, and the principal. Conversations with the school nurse, the social worker, the physical therapist, aides, and the interpreter for Southeast Asian children and parents added data to my collection. When I arrived home each day, I typed my handwritten notes of the day's observations and transcribed my tapes.

Assemblies and Meetings. Throughout the year I attended school assemblies, parent committee meetings, bi-weekly faculty meetings, staff development sessions, administrative meetings, and meetings with guests from other educational institutions. In each of these settings I diagramed where people sat, took handwritten notes of my observations of interactions and behaviors, and often tape-recorded the session.

Interviews. In January, I began formal interviews with teachers, interns, the school secretary, the principal, early-education staff members, and key persons at the school district level—the chief designer of Mega Center's plan and the school board member who initiated the idea for the school. Because of my interest in the development of the schoolwide culture and the use of personal and institutional metaphorical language throughout the building, I interviewed all 16 home-base teachers and a long-term substitute home-base teacher. I also interviewed the four current and past members of the resource team, the two interns, three members of the early-childhood education team whose program was housed in the building, two teacher aides, and two of the office personnel.

In the hour-long, taped, open-ended interviews, I began with a general question, asking the interviewees to reflect on how the year had been for them. Then I moved to more specific topics such as interpretations of the school mission, ideas about teaching and teaching strategies, work with colleagues, and school leadership. I concluded by asking the interviewees to bring up anything else they thought it was important for me to know. During these interviews, persons used a variety of personal and institutional metaphors. After the first four interviews I decided to develop two forms of interview questions to determine if my use of language influenced their responses. I structured the first set of interview questions using language common at Mega Center, for example, Mega Center educator, team members, multiple intelligences, integrated thematic curriculum, vision, vision-keeper, cross-age grouping, and lifelong learning. I designed an alternate interview form asking the same questions using more common educational language, such as teacher, colleagues, students' abilities, lessons, educational beliefs, principal, arrangements of students, curriculum, personal skills, and purposes of education.

Shadowing and Interviewing the Principal. I shadowed the principal for five school days. She arranged for me to sit in a chair off to the side in her office while she worked on projects or made phone calls. Occasionally Suzanne stopped her work to give me background information. She asked each person who came in to meet with her if I could stay for the meeting. Although the agenda for several meetings included sensitive issues, nobody requested that I leave. I followed as the principal moved throughout the building, taking detailed notes on what she did and noting the content of conversations and meetings.

In addition to spending five days shadowing the principal, I interviewed her for approximately six hours. With a tape recorder to capture the conversation, I asked Suzanne questions similar to those I asked teachers as well as questions about her overall view of the school and her reflections on her role as principal.

Discussion Groups with Parents and Students. During May, I conducted focus-group interviews with parents and students. All school parents received an invitation to participate in a focus group. A total of 15 parents met in three one-and-one-half hour sessions arranged at times convenient for them. Parents commented on why they chose Mega Center for their children, opportunities their children had at Mega Center, the school's leadership, and their overall impressions of Mega Center's first year.

The four one-half hour student focus-group sessions occurred during school time. Teachers randomly chose eight volunteers for each session. Children discussed why they came to Mega Center, how their new school was different from their former schools, and what they liked about Mega Center.

Written Materials. Throughout the year I had access to Mega Center's written materials. Each week the school secretary put a copy of *Eagle Notes*, the faculty and staff bulletin, in my mailbox. Teachers gave me newsletters they sent to parents. Occasionally they shared with me letters parents wrote to them. I also examined key documents and a brochure describing Mega Center's philosophy, organizational structure, and programs. A full description of the documents and brochure appears in Chapter 5.

Data collection and analysis were ongoing, simultaneous processes. As preliminary theories emerged from my data, I asked new questions, probed new situations, and sought new perspectives.

Analysis and Reporting

Analysis of my data began early in the participant-observer process. During my first formal visit to Mega Center I heard teachers and the principal describing their roles and discussing the school's programs using language peculiar to Mega Center. The language did not seem to be new educational jargon but evoked unique images of schooling for children. Teachers and the principal used both their new institutional language and personal metaphors. The institutional and personal metaphors of Mega Center's educators became the basis of the coding system I used to analyze my data.

After transcribing nearly 2,000 pages of field notes and interview tapes, I read the field notes and wrote a short summary of each entry. Reading the interview transcriptions, I transferred interviewees' responses on similar topics to 11- by 14-inch sheets of paper, highlighting personal and institutional metaphors with colored markers. Next, carefully rereading the field notes and interview transcriptions, I noted in the margins key words, phrases, events, ways of thinking, and behavior patterns. During a third reading, I made nearly 200 index cards of key words and phrases, citing places in the data where examples occurred. As I arranged the cards in categories, multiple examples of particular metaphors surfaced and certain metaphors and concepts linked with others to form a broader picture. Finally four major metaphors emerged:

1. The vision of Mega Center
2. Families of learners
3. Teams of educators
4. The principal as vision-keeper

These four metaphors are the bases of Chapters 5 through 8.

The story of Jason's maze provides an apt metaphor both for engaging in educational reform and for conducting an ethnographic research study. Changing structures and practices in a school is not a simple task but a complex journey. Mega Center's journey into the educational change process is fraught with false starts, blind alleys, and unexpected turns. At times the story reads more smoothly. Learning from past experiences and open to new possibilities, the school's stakeholders move into the future. The maze seems negotiable.

Studying a school engaged in reforming structures and practices and hence reshaping its culture challenged me both to keep focused and to be open to whatever emerged. The research process was not a straight-line journey. Besides finding both unforeseen detours and unexpected pathways as I read and collected data, I had to negotiate my way through the maze of overabundant transcribed materials to find Mega Center's central metaphors and their impact on the school's change efforts. My method of study mirrors the subject of study. Jason's maze is a metaphor for both.

CHAPTER THREE

Metaphors from History

Reforming education is not a new phenomenon. Many educational historians see three major periods of educational reform in the United States. These include the mid-nineteenth century common school movement, the early-twentieth-century Progressive Era, and the "great ferment of the last generation which as yet has no generally agreed upon name" (Tyack et al., 1980, p. 256). A review of the three major periods of educational reform in the United States forms the backdrop for my study. It reveals the metaphors guiding the thinking and practice of reformers and the politics of reform. A historical review grounds my study by revealing the variety of metaphors shaping discussions of American educational reform.

COMMON SCHOOL MOVEMENT

By the mid-nineteenth century, the common school movement was spreading across the continent in cities, towns, and rural areas. Typically children received their education in one-room schoolhouses. But reformers such as Horace Mann, Henry Barnard, and Calvin Stowe were critical of "school inefficiencies, the ineffectiveness of untrained teachers, a fragmented, uncoordinated curriculum, and scattered schoolhouses with children of all ages jumbled together in one room in American cities and villages" (Cuban, 1988a, pp. 86–87). They encouraged policymakers and educators to restructure educational practices and to initiate graded schools.

Quincy School, the first graded school in the United States, opened in Boston in 1848. It had 8 grades and 12 separate classrooms, each with capacity for 56 students. By 1890, modern graded schools with uniform curricula, textbooks, tests, and promotions from grade to grade appeared in cities across the nation. The common school movement's reform of American education remains today the basic structural arrangement for schooling (Cuban, 1988a).

Common School as Educator of All. The purpose of the common school was to produce "literate, numerate, moral citizens" (Tyack et al., 1980, p. 256). The public would exercise political control and give economic support to the schools. The schools would educate all classes, sects, and ethnic groups, giving them a basic elementary education to prepare them for participating in political life and for entering the work force.

Education as Politics. Reformers had a more subtle purpose for schooling in mind. They believed education was more effective than politics in achieving long-term societal changes (Cremin, 1988). Because education altered traditional relationships among individuals and groups, some saw it as a form of politics. This education-as-politics metaphor would come forward more explicitly with Dewey in the Progressive Era.

The Teacher as Overseer, Drillmaster, Interpreter. Descriptions of classroom activity in the common school suggest metaphors revealing beliefs about how children learn and what they should learn. Barbara Finkelstein's study (cited in Cuban, 1993) of almost 1,000 descriptions of elementary classrooms between 1820 and 1880 found three metaphors for teaching in elementary classrooms. The first metaphor sees the teacher as intellectual overseer who assigned work, punished errors, and required memorization. The drillmaster metaphor applies to teachers who led students orally through the content and required them to repeat lessons aloud, often in unison. The least common pattern reveals the teacher as interpreter of culture. This teacher would explain ideas to the students. Finkelstein found evidence of these metaphors for teaching in all geographical areas of America, in both urban and rural schools, and throughout the time span she studied.

THE PROGRESSIVE ERA

The Progressive Era, with new visions of education, began around the turn of the twentieth century at a time of rapid expansion and continued for the next 50 years. John Dewey represented the more liberal thinking of progressivism, while the more conservative strand derived largely from the work of Frederick W. Taylor (1911) and Max Weber (1947).

School as Factory

Metaphors describing schools in the early twentieth century grew out of the scientific management principles enunciated by Taylor (1911) and the hierarchical bureaucratic model developed by Weber (1947). Top-down decision making and accountability structures, technological solutions to human problems, and the use of quality-control indicators to monitor work characterize this approach (Sirotnik, 1989).

The school-as-factory metaphor appeared in 1916 in the writings of Elwood Cubberley, who described schools as factories and children as raw materials to be formed into finished products. Cubberley believed the specifications for the products came from the demands of the twentieth century. He called for good tools, specialized machinery, and continuous measurement of production to see if it was meeting the standards.

The group of progressives dedicated to efficiency attempted to reform both organizational and ideological structures of education. As their key structural goal, educational administrators sought to centralize control of the urban schools in small boards of education elected at large, give decision-making power to appointed expert superintendents, use state legislatures and departments of education to standardize public education, and consolidate one-room schools. The purpose of the reorganization was to take education away from the decentralized control of lay people, usually ward boards, and give professionally educated superintendents broad administrative discretion. University professors at institutions such as Teachers College, Columbia University, trained and placed superintendents in key educational settings. Educators were confident that the emerging science of education would be a means of shaping social evolution (Tyack et al., 1980).

School as Social Institution

Some progressives rejected the factory metaphor, suggesting that its implementation would produce passive citizens ill equipped to participate in democratic life. Their perception of schooling derived from a different metaphor, the view of school as a social institution. A key figure in this movement was John Dewey, who concentrated his work on articulating relationships between the individual, education, and society. During his tenure at the University of Chicago from 1894 to 1904, his ideas and writings flourished, and he opened his Laboratory School in 1896. In *My Pedagogic Creed*, written in 1897, he set forth his philosophy of education. Dewey defined education as participation of the individual in the consciousness of the race and viewed the school as a social institution designed to immerse children in an embryonic social life especially organized to nurture intellectual, moral, and aesthetic development. He maintained that the subject matter of the school curriculum was nothing more than the accumulated experience of the race and argued that education was the fundamental method of social progress and reform (Cremin, 1988).

Dewey left the University of Chicago in 1904 and became a professor at Teachers College, Columbia University, where he remained until his death in 1952. Here he gained renown as America's most distinguished and influential philosopher of education. In 1916 he wrote his "magnum opus on education," *Democracy and Education*, which describes his conception of democracy and the type of learning environment necessary to support his concepts (Cremin, 1988, p. 172).

Describing how Dewey uses the organic growth metaphor to explain his concept of enculturation, Israel Scheffler (1960) writes:

> Just as living things are different from inanimate things in maintaining themselves by renewal, in reacting to external forces so as to retain their equilibrium with the environment, using these forces as means of further growth, so cultures retain their continuity by reacting to external forces in such a way as to maintain their equilibrium and to grow adaptively and creatively. (p. 53)

Dewey considered education to be the process of transmitting the life of the culture from the group to each new member, guaranteeing cultural continuity.

As he aligned himself with organizations such as the American Federation of Teachers, the American Association of University Professors, and the Progressive Education Association, Dewey's influence grew. By the end of World War II, his progressive philosophy of education had spread throughout the United States.

Despite Dewey's influence, historians of education find it difficult to assess the enduring effects of progressivism and to estimate how teachers implemented progressive methods of instruction in their classrooms. Where there was strong commitment, teachers organized their subject matter using an interdisciplinary approach. Even though implementation of the progressive philosophy and methodologies was limited, the proponents of basics and traditional education found progressives to be at the root of all that was wrong in the public schools. Some historians conclude that progressivism as espoused by Dewey's followers failed to take hold in American education because it became the prerogative of the elite (Stevens & Wood, 1987).

Lawrence Cremin (1988), however, proposes a different view of the fate of progressivism. Near the end of his life, Dewey enjoyed predicting that the time would soon come when progressive education would be so widely accepted as good education that the adjective "progressive" might be dropped. This time arrived following World War II. Although progressivism may not have created the kind of society Dewey envisioned in *Democracy and Education* (1916), it gave the American public the metaphors and accompanying language to debate educational policy and practice.

Three Major Reports

Before moving to the reform movement of the second half of the twentieth century, three major education reports that appeared between 1893 and 1918 and influenced the structure and politics of elementary and secondary schools through World War II deserve attention. In the first report, published in 1893 by the National Educational Association's Commission on Secondary School Studies, the Committee of Ten, under the leadership of Charles W. Eliot, president of Harvard, argued for broader secondary school curricula because of the diversity of students entering high schools in the 1890s. The report called for a "substantial core of academic subjects for all students—those bound for work as well as those bound for college" (Cremin, 1988, p. 232).

Issued in 1895, the report of the Committee of Fifteen directed attention to the "correlation of studies," which emphasized the relationship between curriculum design and the psychological nature of the child. The report reinforced the priority of language studies in the primary grades but shifted the emphasis from memorization to meaning and language. Over 20 pages of the report dealt with teacher training and qualifications.

Twenty-five years after the Committee of Ten issued its findings, the Report of the Commission on the Reorganization of Secondary Education, entitled *The Cardinal Principles of Secondary Education*, urged revision of the common core curriculum, more room for choice among subjects, and increased flexibility in academic subjects. Many school districts already were implementing the report's recommendations, and the testing and sorting of students in comprehensive high schools had begun. Eventually most of the recommendations of these reports became part of the way to do schooling, and by the 1930s systems for student classification and career guidance offered students "blueprints for their futures" (Stevens & Wood, 1987, p. 342).

THE SECOND HALF OF THE TWENTIETH CENTURY

The 1950s began an age of educational conservatism. Themes articulated during the 15 years following World War II still found a place in the reform reports of the late 1970s and 1980s. These included the status of the liberal arts in the curriculum, the efficient use and development of human capital, and the issue of excellence versus equity (Stevens & Wood, 1987).

The Liberal Arts Tradition

Arthur Bestor, author of *Educational Wastelands* (1953), was a strong voice calling for reform in the 1950s and brought educational conservatism and the liberal arts tradition to the forefront of debate. He thought schools should teach students to think and accused educationists of absolving themselves of responsibility for intellectual content in teaching.

With the Russian launching of Sputnik in 1957, a wave of panic hit the shores of America. The education of the intellectually gifted, especially in mathematics and science, became an urgent goal. In 1959, Admiral Hyman G. Rickover prepared an assessment of public education for the House Appropriations Committee. Published in 1963 as *American Education, A National Failure*, Rickover's report said that American education had no clear educational philosophy and no firm objectives. He too called for a strong emphasis on the liberal arts.

The Development of Human Capital

Another strong voice of the 1950s and 1960s was that of James B. Conant, former president of Harvard University. Although he tended to affirm rather than challenge many elements of progressive education, he expressed concern over the weakness of programs for the academically gifted. The recommendations in his report, *The American High School Today* (1959), focused on improving the comprehensive high school by eliminating college preparatory, vocational, and commercial tracks, and developing ability groupings and improving and expanding the core program of basic disciplines such as English composition, science, and languages.

Reform initiatives of the 1950s varied in philosophy; there was no single focus. A report of the Special Studies Project entitled *The Pursuit of Excellence: Education and the Future of America* (Rockefeller Brothers Fund, 1958) acknowledged that the Soviet Union was not the cause of America's education crisis and recommended differentiated curricula for talented students. Debates on educational issues pitted progressive concepts against conservative proposals. During the 1950s, reform proposals "generally saw the two ideals of meritocracy and social utility as serving the larger national good" (Stevens & Wood, 1987, p. 348). The federal government's role in supporting education agendas grew to include 66 categorical programs.

Excellence Versus Equity

The reforms of the 1960s found their grounding in the concept of equal educational opportunity. *Brown* v. *Board of Education* in 1954 had changed the way Americans thought about education and provided a springboard for the movement for equality in education (Cremin, 1988; Ravitch, 1983). People who had been excluded from influence in public education fought for their rights. In 1964, the eighty-eighth Congress passed legislation supporting vocational and technical education and the eighty-ninth Congress extended these commitments in the Elementary and Secondary Education Act of 1965. The 1960s brought not only a wide variety of new programs but also "an 'issue-attention cycle' where people saw others as competitors for attention and funds" (Tyack et al., 1980, p. 260). The American public came to the realization that "in a democratic polity, public education could never be above politics" (Tyack et al., 1980, p. 262).

Reforms of the 1960s continued into the early 1970s and focused on providing equal educational opportunities for students. By the mid-seventies, equity had replaced equality as the major reform word. While equality of opportunity demanded equal facilities, teachers, or curriculum, equity looked at the skills and knowledge the student acquired. This shift became important not only because "it connoted a movement away from the egalitarian democratic ideal" but also because issues of equity and components of quality education merged to form the backdrop for the reform proposals of the 1980s (Stevens & Wood, 1987, p. 348). Reform initiatives in this decade were piecemeal. Teachers and students alike felt pressure to improve, especially in the basic subjects.

The Decade of Reports

The 1980s saw a series of reports berating the educational system for the continuing decline in students' academic performance and linking the nation's economic crisis with low academic achievement. The April 1983 publication of the National Commission on Excellence in Education's (NCEE) report, *A Nation at Risk*, "came to symbolize the nation's dissatisfaction with the quality of public education and its commitment to meaningful reform" (Chubb & Moe, 1990, p. 9). Employing the factory metaphor and viewing teachers as laborers, the report proposed to measure their productivity by testing their students. Capturing the attention of the American public, *A Nation at Risk* was "written in a strident urgent style employing military metaphors reminiscent of the Sputnik era" (Rich & DeVitis, 1989, p. 150). Many states initiated a series of reform measures that they associated with effective education, such as stricter graduation requirements, more homework, and longer school days and years.

The "second wave" of the reform movement began in the late 1980s and includes proposals that would give parents more choice in the selection of the schools for their children, empower and professionalize teachers, and manage schools with site-based structures. While the number and variety of reforms of the late 1980s seem impressive and call for serious changes in school organization, practice, and personnel, "virtually all reforms are cut from the same institutional mold" (Chubb & Moe, 1990, p. 11).

Breaking the Mold

Despite reform rhetoric, the basic structures of American education have remained constant since the mid-nineteenth century. Reform proposals sought to alter educational practices but left intact basic assumptions regarding the purposes of education. Most reform proposals have not challenged the underlying metaphors of professionals or the public.

Moving into the twenty-first century will require educators who are serious about school improvement to consider carefully new school models such as the winning designs supported by grants from the New American Schools Development Corporation. Of equal importance is the work of teachers and principals who will struggle to create new ways to address the needs of the children in their care. As efforts to restructure schools move forward, educators will do well to examine the metaphors embedded in their designs and underlying their new practices.

CHAPTER FOUR

Metaphor, Culture, and Schools

The challenge of transforming schools requires what Elliot Eisner (1991) calls an "enlightened eye," a way of seeing, not merely looking. For example, recognizing the impact an image of schooling such as the factory can have on the lives of students and teachers, we can see intuitively the power of metaphor in shaping school culture. This chapter begins by examining the pervasiveness of metaphor in our lives and in educational literature. It moves to exploring connections between re-forming metaphors of schooling and developing a school culture that supports change efforts.

THE POWER OF METAPHOR

The use of metaphor is pervasive in everyday life, not only in speech but also in thought and action. Based primarily on linguistic evidence, authors and educators George Lakoff and Mark Johnson (1980) argue that most of our ordinary conceptual system is metaphorical in nature, controlling not only our thoughts but also how we negotiate our everyday lives and how we relate to each other. "Since communication is based on the same conceptual system that we use in thinking and acting, language is an important source of evidence for what that system is like" (p. 3).

Understanding and experiencing one kind of thing in terms of another is the essence of metaphor. However, while revealing one facet of a concept, metaphors necessarily hide other aspects. We tend to choose one metaphor over another to achieve coherence within our overall system of thought, expression, and action.

People can and do use metaphorical language because conceptual boundaries are elastic and permeable. Often literal resources are not sufficient to express rich correspondences, interrelations, and analogies for concepts conventionally separated. Metaphorical thought and utterances sometimes embody insights expressible in no other way (Black, 1979).

The use of metaphorical language is an invitation "to explore the context for significant shared predicates—new or old, simple or complex" (Scheffler, 1979, p. 129). Metaphors are like unopened packages (Paprotte, 1985). From another perspective, metaphors are magical because they "allow us to conceptualize and understand phenomena from new perspectives, provide compact imagery of complex things . . . and often guide our attitudes and actions" (Thompson, 1986, p. 4). Thompson suggests submitting metaphors to constant criticism and to dialectical correction and urges comparing rival metaphors by experiment or anecdotalism to evaluate their usefulness.

Lakoff and Johnson (1980) propose that new metaphors have the power to create new reality:

> This can happen when we start to comprehend our experience in terms of metaphor and it becomes a deeper reality when we begin to act in terms of it. If a new metaphor enters the conceptual system that we base our actions on, it will alter that conceptual system and the perceptions and actions that the system gives rise to. Much of our cultural change arises from the introduction of new metaphorical concepts and the loss of old ones. (p. 145)

Understood from these perspectives, metaphor becomes more than a literary device. Through metaphor we organize our view of reality (Ricoeur, 1975/1977). Using metaphorical language, we reveal the meaning we give to our experience. When we espouse new metaphorical concepts, our perceptions and actions undergo change.

EDUCATION AND THE USE OF METAPHOR

Since metaphor is a factor of the human conceptual system, it pervades our thinking not only about our daily life but also about the purposes and practices of education. Alan Tom (1984) describes teaching as a moral craft and points out that some well-established metaphors used in discussions about education such as "hierarchies of needs" and "levels of meaning" strike us as being literally true. Herbert

Kliebard (1972) suggests there are at least three metaphors in the field of curriculum: production, growth, and travel. He explains that each perspective affects both teacher and student. In their book *Understanding the Principalship* (1993), Lynn G. Beck and Joseph Murphy provide a comprehensive study of the metaphorical themes embedded in the practice of school administration from the 1920s to the 1990s.

In *The Language of Education* (1960), Israel Scheffler discusses Max Black's suggestion that the familiar growth metaphor is one that lends itself to the expression of revolt against educational authoritarianism. He also describes the educational metaphors of shaping, forming, and molding. Scheffler cautions against trying to find

> a progressive order of metaphors in education, each more adequate and comprehensive than the last. . . . Educational metaphors in general use are of help in reflecting and organizing thought and practice with respect to schooling, but they are not tied in with processes of experimental confirmation and prediction. (p. 52)

A review of the language of recent reform reports concludes that "the truly reformational reports propose not only changes in the activities of education, but also the language to describe it so that other possibilities can be considered" (Cinnamond, 1987, p. 4). Metaphor provides a powerful tool that "might be invoked profitably by teachers and administrators as a way of reflecting on and possibly improving their own practice" (Mumby & Russell, 1990, p. 120).

Although there is literature describing metaphors that bring to light aspects of teaching, learning, schools, and reform issues, the use of metaphors to frame problems and gain insight into educational issues has received little treatment in the literature (Pugh, 1987). In reporting the results of his study, Wesley Pugh describes gathering metaphors of school administrators and using them as one way to understand and describe what takes place in schools. He suggests his methodology might be useful in understanding and describing other aspects of school life.

RE-FORMING METAPHORS OF SCHOOLING

Educational literature provides a rich variety of examples of how researchers have studied school culture and reform issues using ethnographic methodologies (Goodlad, 1984; Johnson, 1990; Kidder,

1989; Lightfoot, 1983). These and other studies provide readers with a glimpse of how critical examinations of current values, beliefs, and practices in education are giving rise to new metaphors about schooling. In addition, persons involved in restructuring schools are beginning to recognize the significance of metaphor as a lens for viewing what is happening in schools (Preskill, in press).

A Nurturing School

How well American students do on tests is a popular yardstick for the effectiveness or goodness of the nation's public schools. For Sara Lawrence Lightfoot (1983), the effectiveness of schools is a much more complex issue. It involves a mixture of parts producing a whole, including people and structures, relationships and ideology, goals and intellectual substance, as well as motivation and will. These good schools have a "sustained and visible ideological stance that guards them against powerful and shifting societal intrusions" (p. 25). Good schools develop different ways of expressing kind and consistent regard for teachers. Lightfoot believes a central metaphor in good schools is nurturance.

Lightfoot found that substantive participation in the structures and processes of education energizes teachers. Teachers stand at the core of education, shaping what they teach, deciding how to teach it, and determining in what context they will pass it on to students. Teachers feel nurtured and grateful when relieved of clerical, supervisory, or maintenance tasks, but want to feel part of something larger than their own classroom. "Deprived of this wide angle on school culture, deprived of collegial interactions, teachers grow dull" (p. 339).

Lightfoot's conclusions match the findings of researchers Michael Rutter, Barbara Maughan, Peter Mortimore, and Janet Ouston (1979), who elaborate on the meaning of the nurturance metaphor. Teachers not only want to have a part in the school's decision-making process but also need to trust the colleagues whom they choose to represent their views and opinions. For this to happen, teachers need to feel part of a group whose values they share. Also significant for teachers is having adequate clerical help. Teachers see this as a sign that schools take personnel needs seriously.

New Working Relationships

Susan Johnson's findings concur with both Lightfoot's (1983) and Rutter et al.'s (1979). For serious reform to occur, Johnson (1990) believes that teachers' roles must change. Teachers must shed meta-phors derived from industrial models of schooling and "venture be-yond their classrooms, fashioning new working relationships with their peers, and participating in decisions about their schools. As a group they must become accountable for teaching standards and professional performance" (p. 341).

Johnson explains that the first wave of regulatory initiatives in the 1980s made teachers the objects of reform. This posture had the nega-tive results of evoking anger and resistance in teachers and also failed to increase test scores. The second-wave strategy transferred more authority to teachers, making them the agents of change and giving them more control over their work.

At the conclusion of her study, Johnson enumerates five general recommendations. She states that reform measures directed toward these recommendations would make schools the work places teach-ers seek. The new work-place metaphor would address the needs of the school community and improve the quality of education for chil-dren. Adequate funding heads the list of recommendations and decen-tralization follows. Decentralization would make the school site the "primary unit of organization so that teachers, principals and parents can institute practices that address the needs of the school commu-nity" (p. 334). Johnson calls on policymakers to abandon their old metaphors for schooling and asks them to "redirect their attention to improving teaching and learning for inquiry and higher order think-ing" (p. 335). Johnson urges public school staff to engage parents meaningfully in the education of their children. Finally, she challenges schools to grant teachers more influence on what they teach and how their schools run.

Education as Dialogue

Two different approaches to teaching evoke competing meta-phors. If the teaching and learning process is transmission, the ideal educational methods should be capable of successful delivery inde-pendent of individual differences in teachers. If dialogue or conversa-tion is the principal metaphor, education takes place within a personal relationship. Teachers and learners become partners in the educational dialogue (Tiberius, 1986).

Describing four different types of dialogue—dialogue as conver-sation, dialogue as inquiry, dialogue as debate, and dialogue as instruc-tion—Nicholas Burbules (1993) reminds readers of the educationally beneficial and educationally detrimental forms each of the approaches to dialogue can take. He refers to dialogue not as a method of instruction but as an open-ended process and urges teachers to employ flexibility and pluralism in their dialogical approaches.

Education as dialogue has its roots in the Socratic dialogues in ancient Greece. Dewey (1916) also embraced the concept of dialogue, arguing that communication is essential within and across social groups to maintain and strengthen the fabric of a democratic society. But the idea does not appear in the improvement of teaching and learning literature until the late 1970s. It surfaced as a reaction to the manipulation of people and things associated with the transmission metaphor.

Author and educator John Goodlad's findings (1984) confirm the work of his colleagues in the research field. Although schools differ, schooling everywhere is very much the same. The metaphor of teacher as intellectual overseer prevails. Rarely, he says, do teachers abandon

> lectures, quizzes, textbooks, workbooks, and written exercises in favor of learning organized almost exclusively around observation of things outside of schools, projects requiring small group collaboration, and primary documents—with reading, writing and dialogue emerging out of such activities. (p. 265)

Decentralized Structure

Like Johnson (1990), Goodlad (1984) believes that "schools will improve slowly, if at all, if reforms are thrust upon them" (p. 31). He recommends that school districts decentralize and give authority and responsibility to principals, teachers, and parents at the local school site. He paints a picture of "every tub on its own bottom, each with a strong link to the superintendent and to the other tubs in the system" (p. 318). Goodlad sees the individual school as the unit of improvement. Schools should make their own major decisions. The district will prosper "to the degree that its schools exhibit good health" (p. 318).

The images conjured up by these and other studies provide ways of imagining schooling from new perspectives. A vision of a nurturing environment in which respectful and empowering relationships are the norm suggests a familial culture. Education as dialogue moves toward a community-of-lifelong-learners image. Decentralized structures call for envisioning alternative power bases. Such dramatic change from prevailing practice requires not only examining how metaphor both shapes and reflects beliefs and actions but also looking at how change affects organizational culture.

DEVELOPING CULTURE

Culture comprises the intertwining of assumptions, values, and beliefs from which a group's norms, practices, rituals, and meaning emerge. Culture grows not only from early group experience but also from the critical role leaders play, especially in the group's formative stages.Edgar Schein (1992) articulates areas around which a group develops shared assumptions. He identifies assumptions about identity and mission as central elements of a culture. In addition, a group generates assumptions regarding its goals, the means it will use to attain the goals, the criteria it will use to measure how well it is doing, and the correctional strategies it will use if it is failing to meet its goals.

In the early stages of a group's formation, the group relies on the founder's or leader's assumptions, since the group has not yet reached consensus on its shared assumptions. A group's early experience of success or failure forms the basis for its cultural assumptions. As a group works together, members try to reduce uncertainty, and certain values are gradually transformed into "nondiscussable assumptions supported by articulated sets of beliefs, norms, and operational rules of behavior" (Schein, 1992, p. 20).

Individuals engage in the complex and multifaceted process of becoming a group as they deal with the issues of language, boundaries, power and status, intimacy and friendship, rewards and punishment, and ideology (Schein, 1992). Explicit negotiation of these issues is critical to an organization's survival and growth. Schein explains:

> If internal issues are not settled, if people are preoccupied with their position and identity, if they are insecure, if they do not know the rules of the game, and therefore cannot predict or understand what's going on, they cannot concentrate on the important survival issues the organization may face. (p. 93)

Typically, in the early stages of its development a group has a low tolerance for ambiguity and looks to its leader to reduce anxiety. A skillful leader recognizes this phenomenon not only as an opportunity to relieve pressure from individuals but also as an occasion to articulate values and beliefs.

A leader plays a significant role in embedding and transmitting the culture of a group. One of the most powerful ways to discern what is of value in an organization is to observe where a leader systematically or regularly puts energy or attention. Other ways a leader plays a primary role in embedding a group's culture include how the leader reacts to crises, allocates resources, models behaviors, distributes rewards and status, and selects or retires members (Schein, 1992). Through exercising daily actions and articulating beliefs, values, and assumptions, a leader has a powerful influence on the growing culture of a group.

METAPHOR AND CULTURE

Metaphors inform the way in which persons express their assumptions, beliefs, and values. They are vehicles through which individuals express the meaning of experience. They shape policy and practice. Metaphors are prisms on reality.

Culture begins to develop when a leader brings a group together to articulate a vision and share a mission. Not only the leader, but each participant brings personal assumptions, beliefs, and values about the vision and mission to the enterprise. As they negotiate their way through the maze of their identity as a group, they will be speaking and acting out of the metaphors they brought with them to the organization.

Uncovering the assumptions that define the developing culture is an ongoing challenge for both leaders and group members. Demystifying the metaphors giving shape to practice is a second and related process. These processes not only inform individuals about their beliefs, values, and practices but also assist a group in developing its identity. How well the vision takes hold and how effectively the mission is accomplished depends to a large extent on the attentiveness the leader and group give to breaking open their metaphors and consciously reflecting on their developing culture.

The story of Mega Center for Learning's first year reveals how teachers, principal, and parents worked diligently to put in place an educational model that taps the potential of each child and holds high expectations for each child's success. As the year began, they wholeheartedly embraced ways of doing schooling that require modifying practices, changing roles, and altering relationships. They set forth on a journey through a maze that required them to transform their personal metaphors and to develop a collaborative organizational culture. The next four chapters describe how Mega Center stakeholders negotiated their way through the maze of re-forming a school.

CHAPTER FIVE

The Vision

In large, bold type on the front of the brochure Mega Center developed during its first year are the words "Mega Center for Learning . . . Education with a Vision." Whether one defines vision as a revelation with prophetic or mystical character, as highly imaginative insight or foresight, as the ability to conceive what might be attempted or achieved, or as the exercise of sight or the ability to see, vision retains its personal and individual quality. While personal vision guides an individual, shared vision gives an institution vitality and intensity (Senge, 1990). Formation of a shared vision for a school is a dynamic and interactive process requiring leadership from the principal and cohesiveness from the staff (Bennis & Nanus, 1985; Miles, 1987).

Each person who came to Mega Center brought mental images and pictures, based on personal beliefs, of what the school would be and could become. These personal metaphors about schooling inspired some individuals to give unbounded energy to making their images of Mega Center become reality. For others, the discrepancy between their vision and the practice produced ongoing conflict and tension. Their energies focused on serving the children well while personally surviving the year.

Whether or not an individual "had the vision" became a topic of both self-examination and gossip. For many Mega Center teachers, the vision represented not only new ways of thinking about how children learn along with methods and programs exemplifying this thinking, but also deep personal commitment to work toward that vision. Others stated their understanding of the vision differently. They saw the vision as making Mega Center for Learning a worldwide model of excellence. This chapter explores Mega Center's institutional vision in relationship to the personal metaphors of its educators.

EMERGENCE OF MEGA CENTER

Mega Center's beginnings stretch back to the mid-1980s when its home district was enlarging its magnet program. Frances Mayer, a member of the district's school board, was grappling with how the district could do more for its children. She believed that all children could do better than they were doing. Frances was convinced that expectations for children were not high enough and that children were not meeting their potential. She wondered whether building a school around research findings on how children learn and making it a place that promotes positive self-esteem as a prerequisite to learning could strengthen education for children. Frances believed that the key, especially for children who were not doing well, was to find something they really felt good about and build them up in that area so experiences of success would generate feelings of self-esteem and positive attitudes toward learning.

With this basic philosophy, Frances visited one of the district's magnet schools, Valley School for Gifted and Talented, where admissions criteria included testing to meet entrance requirements. At Valley School she attended a session at which teachers taught parents about Bloom's taxonomy and higher-order thinking skills. Frances observed in classrooms where teachers were, as she put it, "drawing children out and respecting everybody's ideas and giving time to think." Frances walked away from Valley School more convinced than ever that those kinds of techniques would be helpful for almost all children, helping them become more independent learners and building confidence enabling them to become lifelong learners.

Frances presented to the school board and the city's north-side community a proposal for a magnet school similar to Valley but without entrance requirements; however, the community preferred having a communications magnet in their area. Frances was disappointed. She had the proposal, which she described as a simple but powerful concept, all on one piece of paper. She put it away and waited for the next opportunity.

The opportunity arose in 1989. The district had space needs and acquired an additional building. Frances pulled out the piece of paper, and this time, instead of bringing it directly to the board and the community, she met with district staff members to find out what they thought. Frances wanted to know "if they thought from their perspective that it was something that would be important, could be successful, would be good for children, might improve the learning, would be replicable . . . if it was a popular concept." Staff members affirmed

Frances's idea, brought their own vision and professional expertise to the concept, and started working on it.

One of the persons at the meeting was Paul Elson, director of staff development for the district. Paul took the lead in fleshing out Frances's idea and developing the Mega Center program. As one Mega Center staff member later described it, "He literally took over and became the architect of the program. He developed the concept." Throughout the school's first year he functioned as consultant, troubleshooter, supporter, sounding board, staff developer, and encourager.

Meanwhile, Frances talked to board members and the community about it. "Somehow," she said, "it took on life through the process . . . so by the time the board had to make a decision about what would go into that building, there was excitement about this from a lot of different directions."

Even before the board made a formal decision to bring Mega Center into being, commitment to the vision and energy to implement the vision were growing. Frances had articulated and communicated her vision. She saw what the new school could look like. She also realized the need to have a shared process for initiating the implementation of the vision. With her leadership, vision building began. In *The New Meaning of Educational Change*, Michael Fullan (1991) discusses vision building as a sophisticated and dynamic process. Frances had an innate sense of the complexity of building a shared vision.

FOUNDATIONAL PRINCIPLES

Foundational principles form the basis of Mega Center's structures and practices. An internal document written by district personnel in spring 1990 elucidates the school's underlying assumptions and describes its organization and programs. Those who wrote this document expected that educators coming to Mega Center would share their beliefs and that they would implement the proposed programs. A second document describing Mega Center's program is an application for a grant submitted to the U.S. Department of Education under the Innovation in Education Program. A third publication, a promotional brochure for prospective parents prepared by Mega Center staff in January 1991, lists the school's central features and states its mission. The following description draws material from these three sources.

Children as Learners

Mega Center's designers built the school's structures and programs on their knowledge of current educational research and their
beliefs about how children learn. Acknowledging that children have
varied abilities and talents, the planners maintained that the educator's
role is to identify and nurture children's unique strengths and to lead
them toward peak performance. Attentive to the many ways children
learn, educators must provide rich and stimulating environments and
a variety of approaches to learning.

Mega Center planners also recognized that children develop positive attitudes when they receive encouragement. The school's architects saw that with sustained and meaningful practice children can
form habits useful for learning and living. They believed that high expectations motivate children to do their best work. Convinced that
every child can and will learn, they insisted that highly trained and
committed educators, with the assistance of parents and the community, could guide children to strive for excellence.

Mega Center would be a school for everyone. Unlike Valley
School, Mega Center would have no admissions criteria, nor would
there be testing to place children in levels, tracks, programs, or groups.
The school would serve children from diverse economic tiers and
varied cultural backgrounds.

When enrolling children, parents would sign an agreement to become partners in their children's instruction. Mega Center promised
training for parents in areas such as organizing a home learning environment, designing out-of-school learning experiences, supporting children's efforts, and helping children develop a sense of responsibility.

Another feature of the school program would be service. Each year
every person in the school, both adults and children, would perform
a service project for the direct benefit of others in the community.

Planning for a total enrollment of 240 students, Mega Center's
designers divided the children into four groups called "families of learners." Each family contained 60 children from kindergarten through
third grade. Educators would further divide the children into four
multi-age groups of 15. Children would begin and end their day in these
home-base groups.

Performance Teams of Adults

Each family of learners would work with a performance team of
adults. The performance team, including professional teachers, a learn-

ing specialist, an intern, paraprofessionals, and volunteers, would interact with the same group of 60 children for their first four years of
schooling. After extensive consultation with parents, performance
teams would design learning experiences and projects for the families of learners. Children would collaborate and cooperate with other
students in the learning process. Mega Center's planners saw the
performance team and parents as advocates, supporters, coaches,
catalysts, and facilitators of children's learning.

Mega Center's program would emphasize extensive, ongoing training for performance teams. The school's planners believed that only
when educators receive training based on current research on learning theories, team functioning, and effective teaching methods can they
develop profitable learning experiences for children. The planners
projected that most of this training would occur at the school with the
cooperation and assistance of nearby college and university personnel.

Mega Center's plan required performance teams to model cooperative adult behavior for the students. In addition, the school would
commit itself to teaching, modeling, and providing experiences that
generate "I can and I will" thinking for students. The school's architects
believed that Mega Center's educators could foster beliefs, habits, expectations, and attitudes leading to high achievement for children.

Personal Learning Plans and Assessment

Mega Center's design called for a computerized personal learning plan for each child, developed jointly by the performance team,
the parent, and the student. The plan centered on what the child
would need to learn and what the child would be able to do after the
learning had taken place. Assessment of progress would focus on the
process of learning as well as on the student's progress and performance. A process-folio documenting the student's progress would be
a major part of the personal learning plan.

The performance team would carefully observe each learner
throughout the year. At the end of each year the team would prepare
a spectrum report for the parent of each child. The spectrum report
would be an essay detailing the intellectual profile of the child. It would
contain suggestions for home and community activities for the child
that might foster growth in areas of particular strength or weakness.

Structure of the Day

The structure of Mega Center's day would reflect its proposed
beliefs and purposes. During the morning, students would study tra-

ditional subject areas but in nontraditional ways. Instructional themes would form the basis, and projects would provide the format for learning reading, writing, mathematics, social studies, and science. During training sessions in the summer, teachers chose the 1990–1991 themes: respect, interdependence, celebrations, diversity, communication, and beauty. Subject areas, integrated around the themes, would be interdisciplinary rather than isolated. Students would explore themes in depth and over time. Students' projects would reflect their best efforts. Process-folios would contain the projects and would demonstrate students' continued improvement.

The afternoon would focus on theaters of learning, exploratory activities in the seven areas of intelligence described by Howard Gardner (1985): linguistic, musical, logical-mathematical, spatial, bodily-kinesthetic, interpersonal, and intrapersonal. Adult teams with particular expertise, training, and interest in the dominant form of intelligence around which the particular theater is based would supervise the theater activities. Common to every theater would be performance. Students would have to do rather than simply know.

Summary of School's Focus

Mega Center's grant proposal submitted under the Innovation in Education Program provides a summary of the school's focus:

> Mega Center for Learning will exemplify the latest and best in human learning and development. This ungraded, performance-based school will focus on four concepts:
>
> 1. EQUIPPING students with the skills needed for future academic success. These will include, yet go beyond, "traditional" basics and emphasize the beliefs, habits, attitudes, and expectations necessary for excellence.
> 2. EXPECTING the best that all people involved in the school have to give. This will include learners, parents, teaching staff, support staff, and administration. We expect excellence.
> 3. EXTENDING present limits to new realities. The Mega Center format will provide extensive development in thinking skills, creative learning, brain-compatible educating [i.e., derived from current scientific understanding of the human brain], and goal setting.
> 4. EXPLORING possibilities, potentials, and premises. We intend to develop and promote a school filled with inquiry, discovery, investigation, risk-taking, innovation, and experimentation. (*K–3 School of Choice*, 1990)

Mega Center sees itself involved in developing new paradigms of teaching and learning that promote learner empowerment. Its brochure, prepared in January 1991 for parents considering enrolling their children in September 1991, asks "What Makes Mega Center Different?" Following the answer, "merging together all of the research shown to enhance learning," the brochure lists seven characteristics of the school:

1. Cross-age grouping of K-4 students with the inclusion of special education students in cooperative/collaborative learning;
2. Whole-language approach to communications;
3. Experiential and activity-centered learning;
4. Thematic, integrated curriculum based on themes chosen by the faculty rather than textbooks;
5. Close and explicit relationship/partnership with parents and the community;
6. Children remaining with teachers for an extended period of time—up to four years;
7. Use of Howard Gardner's (1985) seven intelligences and focus on Dorothy Rich's (1988, 1991) MegaSkills: motivation, common sense, confidence, effort, problem solving, initiative, responsibility, perseverance, team work, and caring.

Changes in Program Components

Recognizing that Mega Center's internal descriptive document, its grant proposal, and its brochure address different audiences and that the three printed pieces use different formats, still it is noteworthy that two features emphasized in the first two documents are missing from the brochure: performance teams and process-folios. These omissions reflect the experience of the first half of Mega Center's first year.

The first omission occurred even before the beginning of the school year when the metaphor of performance team shifted. With performance dropped from the expression, the word *team* conjured up images and practices of prior experiences for Mega Center's teachers. They measured their Mega Center experiences of teaming against old metaphors. Many found a gap between expectation and practice. Chapter 7 addresses how this metaphor shift affected practice.

Mega Center struggled with the second issue, student evaluation, throughout the year. Committed to the concept of evaluation as an ongoing process in which teachers, students, and parents participate,

Mega Center teachers could not find preexisting printed models for evaluation. Process-folios would serve this purpose, but with time and energy already stretched to the maximum, nobody could take on the responsibility of coordinating the effort. The implementation of process-folios would have to wait for another year.

SHARING THE VISION

Even when there is a written, clearly articulated vision for a school and commitment to its implementation by the district, the internal process of developing a shared vision and understanding the complexity of putting the vision into practice must be acknowledged. Top-down initiatives and bottom-up participation must blend intricately for multilevel reforms to be successful (Marsh, 1988). Preconditions that affect the development of shared vision are: "The principal must exercise leadership in promoting a vision, but the staff must also be cohesive enough to be willing to buy some shared set of goals" (Miles, 1987, p. 7). Miles also warns against "tight forward scenarios" and explains that "those steering improvement need good data on what is happening and the capacity to take advantage of unexpected developments in the service of the vision" (p. 13). Chapter 8 discusses the relationship between Mega Center's vision and its vision-keeper. The remainder of this chapter describes the extent to which Mega Center educators developed a shared vision during the school's initial year.

The New Educator

As the implementation of Mega Center's vision required more and more interaction, cooperation, and collaboration of teachers with one another across the school, school life became more difficult and stressful. Mega Center teachers were dynamic people, successful in their previous teaching experiences, and highly regarded by peers and parents. As one teacher expressed it, they were "high-flying people pulled together for this project."

During their August training sessions they engaged in spirit-building exercises. For example, one day at lunchtime teachers drew a letter of the alphabet from a hat and received $2.50 with directions to buy only items beginning with that letter to get lunch for themselves and to buy something to share with others. Accustomed to thinking outside prescribed boundaries, teachers decided to pool their money, to have a potluck lunch, and to interpret the notion of food items beginning with a particular letter as including food groups beginning with the letter. For example, the letter *P* would include both pickles and produce. Groups of teachers went shopping together at local supermarkets. After buying provisions for everyone, they brought back 17¢ in change. Reflecting on this experience, Suzanne Dawson commented, "When I saw the energy and ingenuity of the group, I knew Mega Center would be successful even though we had modest funding at our disposal. We would need to call on this kind of creativity time and time again." This experience reminded one of the teachers of something she remembered from a previous training session: "We are all faced with brilliant opportunities disguised as impossible situations."

Their "we can and we will" attitude continued through the training phase. However, many teachers expressed impatience with training that focused on developing a collaborative culture among themselves and cooperative attitudes among children. They felt they had sufficient expertise and experience in these areas and were anxious to move on to the nuts-and-bolts of how to implement thematic learning with cross-age groupings of students. They were eager to implement their visions of what school could be for children. They did not realize the diverse elements in their own visions regarding schooling for children nor did they recognize the importance of developing a shared vision of what school could be for the educators. The affirmation they felt because of their selection as participants in a new project, which they hoped would become "a worldwide model of educational excellence," carried the day. In the emotion of the moment they forgot even their own more mundane reasons for choosing to apply for positions at Mega Center.

Most Mega Center teachers came from various schools throughout the district. More than half the staff said they applied for positions at Mega Center because they wanted or needed a change from where they were. Some were tired of their jobs or weary of teaching the way they were "supposed to." Others were frustrated and bored or felt stuck, trapped, in a rut, or tired of working alone. Some saw coming to Mega Center as an opportunity for a shift in career emphasis, especially moving from exclusively special education classrooms to an inclusionary regular education model. Some were eager to move to Mega Center because of the convenience of being close to home. A few said they received phone calls asking them to apply. These personal disclosures reveal the need these teachers have for meaningful and challenging work, along with some unformed visions of what this new venture might entail.

Several teachers who expressed their interest in Mega Center as a "change from" also talked about a "change to," exposing their visions of what Mega Center would be. Their visions ranged from very generic to quite specific. Some wanted something new or had creative ideas and thought they could do more at Mega Center. Others mentioned specific program components that drew them to Mega Center: gifted-education orientation, individualization, multi-age groupings, addressing multiple intelligences. A few cited the opportunity to work with Suzanne Dawson as a major reason for applying for a position at Mega Center. Only two mentioned an eagerness to work closely with other teachers.

Some teachers talked about their philosophical agreement with Mega Center's vision. "For many, many years I have believed that Mega Center's vision is what education should be," stated one teacher. Another said she relished the opportunity of being in an alternative school that was "on the cutting edge." She talked about how vital it was to her that a school be attuned to current research and place emphasis on important issues that improve learning rather than on bandwagon approaches and pet projects. "I have a dream inside me," said another teacher, "and this school's holistic tone with whole language and thematic teaching matched my dream."

However formed or unformed their visions of Mega Center were, these teachers saw schooling differently from the traditional factory metaphor for education. In none of Mega Center's classrooms would desks be in straight rows. Bells would not mark the beginning and end of each school day. Children would not spend most of the day sitting in one place, reciting facts, filling in worksheets, writing answers to questions, or taking tests and quizzes. Teachers would not be isolated in their classrooms doing their teaching behind closed doors.

As committed as Mega Center teachers were to changing the educational paradigm for students, they struggled all year to come to new conceptualizations and metaphors for their roles as educators. Many said they felt pressure to implement Mega Center's vision while recognizing growing divergencies among themselves not only about how to implement the vision but also about the meaning of the vision itself. For most, the "We can and we will" attitude of the honeymoon stage reverted to an "I can and I will" pledge to do the best for students. Mega Center's teachers had to grapple with new metaphors for their roles in the context of the school's vision.

Mega Center's foundational descriptions called for teachers to assume new roles. No longer one teacher with one class, the new educator would be part of a performance team. No longer the giver of information, the new educator would guide children's learning. No longer teaching subjects in isolation, the new educator would interact with other educators in the building planning interdisciplinary experiences for the learners. No longer would music, art, and physical education specialists provide preparation time for teachers. All teachers would integrate music, art, and physical education experiences into the day-to-day curriculum. Instead of specialists, four additional teachers with general backgrounds would form a resource team and collaborate with the other teams of educators, providing interdisciplinary options for children. Even as the school year was about to begin, the vision of "the new educator" remained unfocused. An incident illustrating this lack of focus occurred, causing frustration and pain that lasted for the remainder of the year.

The Resource Team

In July, like other teams of teachers, the resource team set about planning how it could provide children with learning opportunities that would stimulate their interest and challenge their potential. Basing its design on Mega Center's vision of organizing curriculum around the needs of the children and providing choices for them, the resource team presented the plan to the teaching staff in late August. The plan not only provided release time for teachers but also gave a different slant to education for the children. The four resource-team members, knowing about the focus on whole language and math in the regular classrooms each morning, had outlined instructional modules integrating art, music, and physical education experiences with science and social studies, using an interdisciplinary, thematic, and seasonal approach. Students would have a choice from a menu of offerings. The children in each family of learners could sign up for a module for a period of time.

But home-base teachers wanted more control. They wanted to be assured of regular preparation times. They also thought the children would be too scattered and would not know where to go. They roundly rejected the resource team's proposal. Home-base teachers' preference for having the resource team act as curriculum area specialists, instructing teacher-assigned groups of students at regular times each week, came out in the testy discussion.

Resource-team members felt professionally undermined. "We had no say in the curriculum plans of other teams," one resource-team member lamented, "but everyone could shoot down our plans." Although hurt by harsh criticism, the resource team agreed to redesign their plan. Unbeknownst to them, other teachers began to draw up a design for the resource team's role, as did a parent. These other proposals were presented to the entire teaching staff, who voted on what the resource team should do for the year.

Continuing criticism put such strain on two resource-team members that they requested transfer from the team. Although they remained in the building for the remainder of the year, the wound of mistrust never healed. These two teachers served as tutors for individuals or for small groups of children. The two teachers who continued as resource-team members worked with classes of students when teachers requested their assistance, sometimes teaching an art or science lesson, sometimes doing team teaching with a home-base teacher. They also designed and coordinated an enrichment program called Travelogue, in which parent and community volunteers shared their expertise with the children in each family of learners.

In their decision-making process, the principal and teachers missed an opportunity not only to build a culture of trust leading to cohesiveness early in the year, but also to implement a new educational paradigm shaped around Mega Center's assumptions and to build alternative metaphors for schooling. Shared vision leading to consensus on this issue would have required the two elements prerequisite to shared vision: leadership of the principal in promoting the vision and willingness of the staff to adopt shared goals (Miles, 1987). Although the inexperience of Mega Center's principal and the lack of cohesiveness of Mega Center's staff may have prevented a critical change from happening, another factor deserves consideration: whether Mega Center's teachers understood adequately the implications of the school's foundational assumptions.

Commitment to Students

When asked in interviews for this study to reflect on their vision of what Mega Center might look like in the future, most teachers talked about present practical shortcomings of Mega Center. Many of their remarks centered around what more could be done for the learners. Others contrasted the positive culture for children with the negative climate for teachers. Though most were slow to praise themselves or their colleagues until specifically asked to recall times when they and the students were caught up in a learning experience, a few commented on the exceptional opportunities children have each day.

One teacher envisioned Mega Center as being in the forefront nationally for teaching children how to think critically and to solve problems in every area, including math. She saw the format of *Odyssey of the Mind*, an international creative problem-solving competition, as a microcosm of how she wants to teach and what she wants for Mega Center: "It's the questions we ask, not the answers, that are important," she said. In expanding these ideas, she revealed her metaphors of teacher as facilitator and coach.

In contrast, another teacher said that Mega Center is below her ideal because there are not enough educational opportunities for children. She likes the thematic approach to teaching, but wants more "meat and potatoes" in the curriculum. She said she has no idea of Mega Center's overall philosophy but sees that it has "all these little components." Her expression of fragmentation stands in sharp contrast to her work with children in the classroom. There she not only maintained an active yet orderly atmosphere, but she used metacognitive techniques, making children aware of what they did and how they thought. Though she helped children build meaning, she could not build a meaning system for herself.

When asked what Mega Center might look like five years from now, a teacher responded, "I don't know . . . I don't know what tomorrow's going to look like." Her feelings of powerlessness and lack of control revealed themselves as she continued, "and they're going to change the whole setup for next year."

Another teacher expressed her affirmation of Mega Center's vision and talked about how she would enhance the practice. "I believe in the inclusion of special education students," she said, "and thematic instruction is a fantastic concept. The parent involvement is working as well as the parent and kid empowerment. . . . But I want more student choice and more parent involvement in the learning process." She summed up her understanding of Mega Center's vision: "Once we walk through the doors we are saying the traditional is not in our realm, and it can't be our security blanket. The school isn't the walls." Her remarks echoed those of district office personnel who expressed the belief that the key to transforming education is getting educators to think differently.

Another teacher, immediately focusing on the students, said she wants Mega Center to "disprove skeptics" and "be a dynamite place where kids are free to be themselves and really expected to just go-go-go, but in a nurturing setting."

In contrast, still another teacher expressed her disagreement with Mega Center's vision, her disenchantment with its practice, and her disengagement from the process of schoolwide improvement. "They talk like there's an educational utopia out there . . . it's pop psychology . . . the language they're using and all the fancy words mean absolutely nothing. They look good on paper, but it's all recycled. A worldwide model? They're not doing it." She expressed her own understanding of the role of a teacher by comparing it to the role of a mother. "Children are nurtured in my classroom," she said.

Several teachers expressed their images of Mega Center's vision simply: "Helping people achieve their personal best"; "Students learning the way they learn best"; "Happy children, excited about learning, real at-task, and feeling good about themselves . . . children excited about learning . . . lifelong learners." The immediate focus on children and an integrated, thematic, nurturing learning environment reflects what outsiders would see as they toured the building.

One teacher, Ken Stowe, described in detail how he believes he put Mega Center's vision into practice when he used Gardner's (1985) theory of seven intelligences in planning a thematic, integrated experience for his students: "I know I've hit a nerve in their learning when they come up to me and ask if they can do a project again," he said. "This happened when we did a project in preparation for going on an overnight to Greendale Woods." All the children in Ken's family of learners stayed in their multi-age home-base groupings during the entire morning for two days. Ken told his group they would build a model of Greendale Woods from a map he would give them. At first they had no materials. Divided into three cooperative-learning groups, the children could get resources to build their model by working and earning money to purchase materials at the World Store. The store had limited resources. The children could earn money by doing activities such as reading, showing teamwork, writing or performing songs, and demonstrating physical exercises. First, the students met as a group, to decide what they needed, to find out how much it cost, and to plan how to make enough money to purchase their materials. After buying the resources, the group began building its model. They needed to organize their facts about Greendale Woods and carefully plan a model that included cabins, paths, and a farm. "There was a flow of commerce, earning of money, and being limited in resources," Ken said. "If the store ran out of resources, they could trade with other teams to get what they needed. It was exciting to see the models go up and the children work in teams. It was like having a . . . microcosm of a social system develop." Ken explained the role of the teacher as helping students to see patterns and to make connections.

Cohesiveness of Staff

Many teachers expressed disappointment at the dissonance between their vision of how they expected the staff to relate to one another and what was actually happening. "I'd like to see us working together for the students, not at one another's throats; fired up, not nit-picky," commented one teacher. Another wanted to focus on creating a warm atmosphere for the children "regardless of what's going on internally." Another said, "We need to work together. I was hoping this would be different." Still another said, "I wouldn't have anticipated the conflict." Another stated it even more strongly: "It just seems to be quite virulent around here."

One teacher expressed her need to develop a sense of shared vision: "I see this as a place where every learner has the opportunity to do his or her personal best, but it still feels real 'loose-endy.' I need more of a feeling of centeredness or focus."

Several teachers said they had stopped talking about issues on which they disagreed. "It's almost like if you're not 100 percent party line, you're suspected of losing the vision," lamented one teacher. Likewise, teachers had few opportunities to explore areas of agreement. Meetings focused on practical matters and announcements. Time for individuals to explore their own metaphors of schooling did not exist. Sometimes in the press of time, decisions flowed not from the persuasiveness of the evidence, but from expediency.

Although there was a parent lounge in the building, there was no staff lounge or comfortable place where teachers gathered to relax or to share personal and professional stories. One teacher said, "We have four schools within a school." But teachers in two of the groups had major conflicts before school started or early in the school year. Mega Center was not ready to explore personal metaphors about schooling and sharing a vision about education. This would have required, first, building a basic level of staff cohesiveness.

Two staff meetings, one early and one later in the school year, exemplify efforts made to develop staff cohesiveness and to help Mega Center's teachers work together as a whole staff. Already in late September staff members were at odds with one another. Decisions had to be made about how teachers would get their preparation time. Fearing that protection of self-interest would compromise the vision, Suzanne Dawson invited one of Mega Center's planners, Paul Elson, to begin the staff meeting. Paul talked about Mega Center as a magnificent idea.

People need ideas that are bigger than they are. And I think if
you look historically, when human beings like us, frail, insig-
nificant, weak, with shortcomings and egos, when we struggle
and have problems is when we let ourselves get bigger than
the idea we represent. . . . And Mega Center is a big idea. And if
it fails it's not going to be because it wasn't a good idea. It's
going to struggle because the people are getting in the way of
the idea. And sometimes we've got to have the wisdom to back
off to the side and let the idea take center stage. If we keep the
idea in the spotlight and we become the guide on the side, it
will work. But if we become the sage on the stage it's going to
struggle. . . . So the idea is the thing to keep coming back to
and what the beliefs are that got us all here together.

Paul emphasized the importance of shared vision and gave staff members practical advice on how to approach persons with whom they
had differences.

Paul's meeting with the faculty occurred at a critical time for the
teachers. Immersed in the time-consuming work of creating their own
curriculum, they had dedicated many evenings and weekends to preparing for the next day. Although they were accustomed to being recognized as excellent teachers by peers, parents, and students, each
was now one among many new teachers. Faced with the challenge of
working as teams, they had sometimes set aside their own preferences.
Many had given up summer vacation plans with their families to attend staff development sessions at Mega Center. Now, Paul asked them
"to back off to the side and let the idea take center stage."

In wholeheartedly committing their energies to Mega Center, the
teachers had made extraordinary sacrifices. Some said their families
suffered. Others had become ill. Fatigue and stress may have triggered
many of the conflicts among them. Through his presentation, Paul
reinforced the teachers' diminishing self-confidence. They left the
meeting wondering if anyone appreciated or valued them personally
or professionally. Despite Paul's efforts, the struggles continued and
intensified.

In March, Sarah Newton, a special education and early-education specialist, conducted a morning session with the Mega Center
staff. The intended plan for the morning focused on learning styles,
but Sarah sensed the group's need to talk about other issues. They
needed time and a safe place to begin creating new visions of their
lives and work together. They would soon begin to plan for a new

year. Many felt exhausted from the difficult work of implementing the vision as they saw it and needed to begin to build connections with one another that would sustain rather than intimidate them when they needed support. They knew Mega Center was a great idea. They worked hard and successfully to bring fresh and creative learning opportunities to the children. They were ready to hear what Sarah had to say about communication and the stages of becoming a community. They were ready to explore a new way of understanding themselves as a group. They were ready to consider a new metaphor for their relationships with one another. They ended the meeting promising to be gentler with themselves and with one another as the year wound down.

VISION AND CULTURE

Initially only those most closely associated with crafting Mega Center's foundational principles understood and espoused the vision. Teachers who applied for positions at Mega Center may have caught glimpses of their own beliefs in what they heard about the new school, but this would not be enough to sustain them in breaking the mold of traditional schooling. They needed time and opportunity to examine Mega Center's founding beliefs in light of their own and to mold programs consistent with those beliefs. Those who would be implementors must also be designers of the program. Developing a vision is an ongoing process that continues throughout the implementation process. While initially relying on the assumptions of the school's designers and leader, Mega Center's culture would take shape as those involved in the day-to-day operations of the school worked together.

Mega Center's planners envisioned principal, teachers, and parents working cooperatively to provide a world-class education for the children. Although committed to this ideal in theory, during their August orientation teachers rejected plans to consider how they might develop a collaborative culture among themselves. Saying they all had experience in working cooperatively with others, they chose to move directly into curriculum planning. However, when faced with their first critical decisions, neither their prior experience in other schools nor their recent successful experience of pooling resources and providing lunch for everyone transferred automatically to professional decision making. For example, in dealing with the resource-team dilemma, rather than developing a collaborative process for coming up with a solution, groups put themselves at odds with one another, each designing proposals that had to stand the test of acceptance by other groups. This situation reinforced a pattern of win-lose decision making and we-they thinking that gained momentum throughout the year.

Even before hiring the teachers, Suzanne Dawson assumed that Mega Center's foundational principles and consequent programs constituted promises to the district and to the community. This belief grew, in part, out of an experience she had shortly after the district superintendent appointed her principal of Mega Center.

On a hot, humid, June day, Suzanne met a prominent business-man in an elevator at the district office. After congratulating her on her new position, he said to Suzanne, "I've got a business card here, and Mega Center ought to do this." Suzanne read the card: "Deliver more than you promise." The businessman continued, "You know, education always talks a big show and always promises a lot. Then what happens? They deliver the same old stuff. Every school should live by what this card says." Suzanne remembered this encounter and re-counted it at a faculty meeting in late September when teachers questioned the wisdom of adding another program component, theaters of learning, to their already crowded schedules.

Her belief that Mega Center must deliver on its promises posed a major barrier to developing a shared vision among the teachers. Teachers gave opinions on how to implement programs without discussing their understanding of how each program helped the school reach its goals. Suzanne felt personally and professionally threatened when teachers challenged her on the purpose or timing of initiating a new program. She was determined that Mega Center would deliver on its promises. Some teachers began to keep dissenting opinions to themselves, while others formed subgroups to cope with the lack of schoolwide consensus.

Creating a new school presents challenges beyond preparing for the events of the next day or week, or even for the next year. It opens the opportunity for educators not only to do things differently but also to think differently. Mega Center's founding principles expected parents, teachers, and principal to assume new roles in the children's education. The burden of meeting day-to-day challenges and the need to stabilize expectations of self and others prevented teachers from reconceptualizing their role as teachers. They engaged in some talk about new roles and responsibilities, but when faced with a situation, they reverted to prior metaphors.

VISION AND JASON'S MAZE

Consideration of a line from the story of Jason's maze sheds light on the relationship between Mega Center's vision and the implementation of the vision. Jason said there were many ways to get through his maze. Like Jason's maze, there was no one way to get from the conceptualization of Mega Center's vision to its implementation. Moving from beliefs and values to practice would be a complex social process. Unaware of this complexity, Mega Center educators hoped to protect the vision and tried hard to put it into practice. They moved into a "tight forward" mode, missing opportunities to share their personal visions and to shape their common vision (Miles, 1987). Absorbed immediately by their practice, they did not recognize the variety of images of schooling each person brought to Mega Center. They assumed there was one vision, one perspective, one metaphor.

Clashes in personal metaphors of teaching and learning produced anger and mistrust. Dissonance between vision and practice brought fatigue and discouragement. Finding time to explore one another's metaphors, with all their differences, could not only enhance the vision but also had the potential of building bridges of communication and trust.

CHAPTER SIX

Families

Mega Center's institutional metaphors highlight people and their re-lationships with one another. The words *family of learners* tripped easily off the tongues of children, parents, and Mega Center teachers. No other phrase appeared more often in the school's written docu-ments. As an adjective, *family* modified nouns such as reunions, meetings, affirmations, and songs. Teachers used the phrase *because we are family* to provide children with reasons for taking turns, shar-ing materials, and speaking respectfully.

FAMILY AS METAPHOR

At the last staff meeting of the year, district staff development director Paul Elson presented his picture of how the family metaphor fits into the scheme of a child's education. To illustrate the growth of the family concept, Paul drew four concentric circles on the black-board. "This is Mega Center's family of learners," he said, pointing to the inner circle, "and perhaps the greatest strength of the curriculum is what you people have been doing all year." He described how he saw Mega Center educators providing a functional family environment and experience for the children. "I think where people are wallow-ing," he explained, "is where they're still under the old thought that kids come to school with some skills that functional families inculcated in the children and that's really not the case for a lot of our kids any-more. A lot of schools are struggling with the fact that kids truly are different than they used to be." He referred to the MegaSkills concept as one of Mega Center's major features, describing these skills as pre-requisites to learning. "I think we can underemphasize a lot of things," he stated, "but that's not one of them."

Paul continued, explaining his vision. The metaphor for school-ing for intermediate-grade students would be a learning community.

Middle-school or junior high students would form a learning society, while the emphasis in senior high school years would be on learning for world citizenship.

School-as-Family

The school-as-family metaphor is not unique to Mega Center. When this image prevails in a school,

> the family metaphor sees each person (student and staff) as a unique individual worthy of respect and dignity in a setting that is emotionally secure and coherent. Accordingly the purpose of school is to create an emotionally healthy social environment that fosters responsibility and mutual respect. (Baker, 1991, p. 35)

The family metaphor is fundamental to education since society requires that school personnel and parents act as co-guardians of children. Even legally, school personnel act *in loco parentis*.

Although parents and teachers sometimes see the needs of children differently, the power of the family metaphor does not diminish. Both teachers and parents have a legitimate claim to the role of nurturing children. A school can authentically refer to itself as family when teachers and staff have genuine concern for the welfare of children and when all staff share responsibility for nurturing children (Comer, 1980).

At Mega Center the principal and teachers considered all adults educators, regardless of their particular roles or responsibilities. These educators consistently expressed their care and concern for children. Teachers focused their energies on giving children full, rich educational experiences that were significant to them in the here-and-now. Aware of the developmental needs of primary-age children, teachers also provided supportive family environments in their classrooms. Children had nooks and crannies where they could go to be by themselves or to talk with a friend. There were corners to play house like grown-ups and spaces to play with toys like children. One teacher described her classroom as a family room where everybody's children liked to gather before the beginning of the school day.

Ten days after the start of the school year, Mega Center held its first gathering of the children and teachers in all four families. Assembled on the floor in the gym, children in each family sang their special family song, recited their own family's affirmation, and watched teachers perform skits portraying the MegaSkills in action. Then, with arms crossed over their hearts, all repeated Mega Center's pledge after Suzanne Dawson: "We, the children, parents, educators, and community members, working together as a family of learners, nurture enthusiasm for lifelong learning. Using our knowledge and understanding, we commit ourselves to excellence!"

Who Belongs

Mega Center's pledge encompassed children, parents, educators, and community members in the family of learners. The complexity of integrating the voices of this broad constituency into the school's daily life presented unique challenges. Chief among Mega Center's stakeholders were the parents. The school's educational plan called for their intimate involvement in shaping their children's education and for setting direction for the future of the school. As parents took an increasingly active part in the school, the professional role of the teachers shifted, at times causing tensions and putting both teachers and parents on the defensive.

Examination of Mega Center's practice reveals, with few single-incident exceptions, consistent regard for the value and dignity of each child. It also reveals the educators' struggles to dismantle the traditional hierarchical notions of boxed-in roles and responsibilities of those involved in schools. Who actually formed the nurturing family was an issue Mega Center had to raise to a conscious level and address.

The Oxford English Dictionary (1989) records a variety of definitions of *family*. The range extends from servants in a household, to everyone in a household, to parents and children (not necessarily living together), to a person's children regarded collectively, to descendants of a common ancestor, to persons bound by religious or political ties, to objects with common features. Just as a monolithic definition of family from which to draw a metaphor does not exist, contemporary membership in and experience of family vary widely. Mega Center's ambiguity in understanding and practice reflects both the many definitions and the varied experiences of families.

The story of Jason's maze provides a conceptual vehicle to consider the school-as-family metaphor. Just as there is no clear and obvious path through a maze, the multiple definitions and configurations of families add to the complexity of designating the composition of Mega Center's families. What appeared to Mega Center's designers as a concept that would draw children, parents, educators, and community together actually led them to dead ends when family was not the operative metaphor. However, the teachers found a way through the ambiguity of the maze as they helped children understand they were family to one another.

FAMILY NAMES

Beginning at the open house before the start of the school year, Mega Center's children identified with their family names, derived from types of trees. One teacher, Bernice Farrell, recounted the story of how the teachers decided on the family names. "During the training sessions in August we had the philosophy of the school posted on a tree, and that's where we got the tree idea," Bernice explained. "It stemmed out of the family tree concept." Bernice recalled parts of the discussion. Families have roots in their ancestors. While children grow, they learn from their parents and grandparents. Mega Center educators now form part of that family tree, fostering growth and learning. "So," Bernice said, "each team of educators chose the name of a tree for its family."

One of the teachers was not present for the discussion and decision. When she returned, she asked, "Why is this a tree school? It sounds like an environmental school. We shouldn't have trees." Bernice explained the response:

> People heard her concern, but did not want to hack this over. There was a lot of time pressure, so we made the family name into an address. The Pine Tree Family became Pine Grove, and each family classroom would bear an address, like mine would be 119 Pine Grove. Then people coming to the school could find the room easily.

In actuality the transfer from family name to address never happened. One teacher's reflection and a staff decision did not alter an already developing metaphor. Children at Mega Center would belong to families bearing the names of trees.

FAMILIES OF LEARNERS

Although the original plan for Mega Center provided for 240 students, heightened community expectations and high parental interest in the school's philosophy and proposed practices resulted in opening enrollment to nearly 400 children. This increase in student population required hiring a larger staff than the planners had intended. Each of the four families consisted of four multi-age classrooms of an average of 24 students. From the very beginning of the year, the family metaphor expressed itself in classroom furniture arrangements, in school-day routines, in conversations among educators, and in teaching and learning experiences.

Arriving at school, children came immediately to their home base, where they played, socialized, or curled up in a comfortable chair with a book until the school day began. Although the term *home base* has baseball connotations, neither children nor teachers spoke of those connections. Home base was the starting and ending place for each day, the place where children could count on seeing familiar faces and feeling at home.

Family Meetings

A family meeting marked the beginning of each day for one family. Other families met occasionally. Teachers modeled and reinforced the family metaphor at these meetings by sharing leadership responsibilities with one another and by giving students opportunities to discuss family issues. Frequently teachers praised or affirmed the children in their family by saying, for example, "Every kid in this whole family is very special."

In one family, lunchroom etiquette needed improvement. Instead of berating the children about their behavior, the teachers used the family metaphor. They urged the children to think of the place where they ate at school not as a lunchroom, but as a family dining room. Emphasizing dining-room manners, the teachers quickly captured the children's imaginations. Soon the children were trying to figure out how they could get the other families in the school to call their school eating place the dining room.

A Nurturing Environment

Mega Center teachers spontaneously used the term *nurturing* in describing their roles in relationship to needs of the children. At a staff meeting, Suzanne Dawson suggested pairing older children with "the little ones who need more nurturing." She was referring to five-year-olds whose parents reported they were overwhelmed by the complexity of long lunch lines. Discussing the whole-language groupings in the family, a teacher commented, "I take the first graders who need some nurturing." Although this teacher still spoke in grade-level language, she recognized the need for an integration of nurturing and teaching.

From an overall perspective, Suzanne Dawson described to visitors her vision of how Mega Center could maintain a nurturing environment for students as they approached the move to middle school. She reported that plans for Mega Center's growth included adding a grade each year so that by school year 1993–1994 the school would have a seven-year program, comparable to K–6 in traditionally structured schools. This framework, she maintained, would encompass Paul Elson's notions of the family-of-learners and the community-of-learners. She said the district planned to initiate a middle-school program in 1993–1994, beginning with sixth graders and adding a grade each year through 1995–1996, at which time the school would include eighth graders. The middle school's organizing metaphor would be society-of-learners. "Kids who are still immature," Suzanne explained, "who still need a lot of nurturing, who may not even be up on skills, could remain in a more nurturing environment for a year before joining the society of learners because there would be twelve-year-olds at both the elementary school and the middle school."

Relationships Among Children

Teachers recognized the benefits of having children arranged in multi-age groupings. "Children help each other and use their own resources first before coming to the adult," commented one teacher. "Cross-age families bring out nice qualities in the older kids," remarked another teacher. "With cooperative learning activities planned into each day, children learn how to work together and be responsible for one another from the very beginning," another teacher said.

Children related their experiences in their families of learners in positive terms. Letitia, an eight-year-old, liked the way older children were able to help younger ones in her family. Jeremy enjoyed getting to know everybody. Thayer is an only child and enjoyed the chance to be with youngsters of different ages. "We really don't have grades," explained Tom, "We make different kinds of friends." Jennifer echoed Letitia's feelings, saying that older children can set an example. Six-year-old Beth said she liked to see what the older students could do. "I've learned a lot from them," she remarked.

The Schoolwide Family

Family meetings, family songs, and cooperative group experiences drew the children in each family together. Schoolwide norms, rituals, and celebrations provided linkages among the families and created a sense of broader family participation. Natural bondings occurred because siblings were sometimes in different Mega Center families. As the year progressed, teachers saw the need to develop schoolwide behavioral norms and consequences for the students, especially for a common area such as the playground. Teachers struggled with how much autonomy they wanted to maintain as a family and how much structure they wanted to accept from the larger schoolwide family.

Each family developed rituals and a rhythm of celebrations. For some, the rituals included daily recitation of an affirmation. For example, one family's affirmation was: "I like myself and what I do, and I'm happy to be here too." After learning about the diversity of the human family and customs and celebrations of other peoples, some families staged exhibitions of dance, art, poetry, and song along with displays of children's multimedia projects. Other families in the school, along with parents, friends, and community members, came to see the results of the children's work and to celebrate their success with them.

A sense of schoolwide pride developed early in the year, beginning with a birthday party for the new school. After singing happy birthday to Mega Center, the children received a small gift and enjoyed cake. Family reunions held throughout the year maintained the momentum of an all-school spirit for the children. Recitation of their school affirmation, "I care about myself and I care about others," together with the quieting-down symbol of crossing their arms over their chests, formed part of the ritual for each reunion. These rituals and celebrations reinforced the children's sense of identity not only with their individual families but with the larger school family.

ADULT FAMILY MEMBERS

Mega Center's children developed a strong sense of loyalty to their individual family of learners and to the schoolwide family. The school's principal, teachers, and staff expressed both in words and in practice their conceptualization of school-as-family for the children. Although the teachers and staff related to children as family, their relationships with one another did not flow from the family metaphor. Neither were parents and guardians of the children viewed through the lens of the family metaphor.

The Educators

When applying for positions at Mega Center, teachers knew the school would be different from others in the district. A main ingredient in making the school different would be the role adults would play.

Mega Center teachers realized the importance of nurturing children and fulfilled that role daily with hugs and words of comfort or encouragement. They recognized that children learn best when they are actively engaged in the learning process. They understood that the teacher was no longer the giver of knowledge and the student the receiver of information. Teachers articulated the importance of both process and product in learning. They talked eagerly and excitedly about their growing understanding of what it means to be a teacher. One teacher expressed the realization of her changing role as she described a situation in which the children challenged one another while learning math: "The old part of me is saying 'Are we wasting time?' and the new part is saying 'Look at those thought processes!'" Sometimes teachers slipped back into their old ways of teaching but soon caught themselves and moved away from traditional practices.

Changing Roles and Relationships. Although Mega Center teachers were finding new words to describe their roles in relationship to teaching children and were using the term *team* to connote their relationship with one another, they employed no explicit language relating themselves to their families of learners. Occasionally a teacher would say, "We are all part of this family," but the relationship of teachers with one another as family members remained unnamed.

The dilemma grew, in part, from Mega Center's change from traditional to new structures of schooling. Staff were accustomed to having one teacher responsible for students in a single classroom, but now four teachers were responsible for a family of learners. This shift in practice caused one teacher to express her experience as a feeling of loss of identity:

One of the most difficult things for me here is feeling that I don't have a solid identity . . . like who I am as a teacher. It seems like it's a little more blurred here. I think I knew that would happen because of teaming, but it has been difficult not to feel quite as acknowledged as I did where I came from. I had a lot of acknowledgment there.

Originally Mega Center had five families. The Cedars consisted only of adults, the resource team. As the year progressed, the family name *Cedars* dropped from usage, and the two remaining members became known exclusively as the resource team. This inadvertent change indicates that before extending the family metaphor to adults, teachers needed new understandings and experiences.

The teachers could not apply the family metaphor to themselves until they developed interdependence, trust, and loyalty. Accustomed to operating as autonomous professionals who gave support to children, the teachers failed to acknowledge their own need for encouragement from one another. Still thinking from hierarchical perspectives, most looked to Suzanne Dawson for affirmation rather than expecting praise from their colleagues within their families. Within some families, teachers experienced more isolation than interdependence. Disagreements on professional issues and gossip about personal matters shut people off from one another. In other families, trust and loyalty grew as teachers gained confidence while sharing personally and professionally.

Family Dysfunction. Experiences and observations of conflict and mistrust caused one educator, Corrie Quinn, to comment, "I definitely would not have the family theme here." She explained that because of the rising incidence of dysfunctional families, by using the word *family* as a description of Mega Center's structural basis, "we are bringing some of that dysfunction in here. . . . Some of the stuff that has happened here is very typical of dysfunctional families." Corrie spoke of one Mega Center family that did not have adequate space in the beginning of the year. "It took an outside person coming in and saying 'look at this' to get it changed. That's typical of families that aren't looking at their own stuff. It's the outside person that comes in and has to make the impact on the family."

Boundary Issues. Other Mega Center teachers implicitly compared the school with a dysfunctional family, citing lack of boundaries as a problem. "It's all enmeshed," said one teacher, commenting on a situation she observed in one family. Another teacher said, "I had a hard time coming this morning because we don't have any boundaries around here. Teachers feel they can come charging right into my room at any time."

Boundaries between parents and teachers also needed clarifica-
tion, according to other teachers. One said, "Parents have been allowed to run the program," while another spoke of the "need for more
refined guidelines for parents and their role in our school." At one staff
meeting, the topic under consideration was the process of including
parents' ideas in decisions about the coming year. One teacher commented to others at her table, "Do parents have ideas! I feel like a piece
of meat. That's what I want to focus on next year—boundaries!"

Handling Conflict. The handling of conflict became another factor
in understanding family dysfunction as a way to describe problems
facing Mega Center. One teacher commented,

> People were not up front because when anyone put an issue
> on the table, it was interpreted as trying to sabotage Mega
> Center. I was putting things on the table because there were
> major problems here, and if we didn't look at them we weren't
> going to make it.

Although several staff development sessions addressed conflict resolution, some teachers thought problems were swept under the rug.
Some placed blame on administration. Others faulted their colleagues,
citing the lack of communication and trust. The possible connections
between their personal and interpersonal struggles and the ambiguity of their new roles in relationship to the family metaphor did not
occur to them.

The Parents

Mega Center promised to create and to maintain close and explicit
relationships and partnerships with parents and the community. The
Mega Center pledge also included parents as part of the family of learners. Parents worked as volunteers in classrooms and special programs.
They organized a science fair for the students. Parents coordinated
fund-raising efforts and set up a school library. Occasionally they
guided prospective parents through the school. A room in the office
area served as a parent lounge.

Individually, teachers worked cooperatively with parents, listening to their concerns and insights regarding their children. In most
cases, trust between parents and teachers grew throughout the year.
When the conversation centered on an individual child, many teach-

ers and parents had experience in relating to one another. The traditional roles of professional teacher and involved parent sustained the relationship.

Contractual Partners. Evidence emerged even before school started that parents were contractual partners in their children's education. The overwhelming interest of parents in the Mega Center program caused the district to double the school's projected enrollment. "One of the major components that really intrigued people in this model is the heavy parental involvement," Suzanne Dawson explained to teachers visiting from a suburban school district. Suzanne continued,

> We have a parent commitment that was developed by the parents during the summer. But people were signing up before that. They just knew there was going to be some kind of parent commitment, agreement, contract that every parent was going to have to sign, and they had no idea of what that was going to be. They bought that as a pig-in-the-poke.

The parent agreement gives parents options on how they will support their children's learning at home, at school, and in the community.

Parent Concerns. Parent involvement at Mega Center extended beyond concern for their own children. Referring to the school's promises, parents pushed for specific programs they knew from their children's former schools as well as for changes in Mega Center's programs. One teacher observed that external pressures were mounting because parents thought this would be the best school in the city. "They didn't leave room for growth pains," he said.

One specific point of controversy arose early in the year. Mega Center initiated the Explore Room, where children went three times a week for 45 minutes each time. Games and other materials and supplies located throughout the room gave children opportunities to explore their interests and intelligences. Interns and volunteers staffed the room.

Parents and teachers conceptualized the purpose of the Explore Room differently, using two distinct metaphors. Many parents saw this experience as free playtime and objected to it as a waste of time. Initially the principal and teachers saw it as an opportunity to learn through play and set up systems for adults to monitor children's choices. The deeper controversial issue was that there were too many children and too few adults in the Explore Room at one time for it to be a high-quality learning experience for the children. Parent volunteers saw this situation, and most teachers acknowledged it.

When parents complained to Suzanne Dawson, she brought the issue to the administrative staff for discussion. The challenge facing the teachers was how to address the parents' concerns while creating a solution that was satisfactory to both parents and teachers. As the teachers discussed the situation, they mentioned two potential remedies: modify the program to satisfy parents as long as it would not revert to the traditional school paradigm, or educate parents through written explanations and skits during the upcoming open house.

Unwilling or unable to alter teachers' preparation-time arrangements to increase the adult-to-child ratio in the Explore Room, some staff members viewed the problem as one of parent perception. The issue became a recurring concern for some parents and a sign that the staff was unresponsive to parent concerns. Parents questioned their place as part of the Mega Center family. Mutual confidence eroded.

Parent Involvement. Despite this issue, parents continued active involvement in the school and forged partnerships on many fronts. Parents and community members researched and recommended to the district school board a name for the building that housed the Mega Center program. Parents developed an evaluation form for Mega Center programs to be sent to parents at the end of the year. Parents and community members shared their special expertise and interests with students in Travelogue, a one-hour, once-a-week enrichment program for the children in each family coordinated by the resource team. Parents actively participated in organizations such as the Parent Teacher Organization, the Parent Advisory Board, and the curriculum committee.

The work of the curriculum committee provides another example of competing metaphors. Even with one teacher and the principal on the committee with six parents, partnership and family metaphors did not prevail in the relationship between this committee and the entire teaching staff. Some parent curriculum committee members saw themselves as providers of programs and opportunities for children as well as overseers of the school curriculum. The parents on the committee generated ideas for programs they wanted to see included in the school and began making plans for implementing their ideas. The teachers lacked sufficient time to discuss how to incorporate these additional opportunities for children into the curriculum. Also, they resented the idea of having parents come into the school to oversee curriculum. Teachers thought this was their professional role.

Parent Perceptions. Reflecting on the differences between their adult experience of the school-as-family and their children's experiences, parents confirmed the sense of family for children. Hannah reported that her son has a strong sense of belonging. On the other hand, although she put in a lot of time and energy at school, she felt she was still outside the creative process. Patty said she would feel more a part of the school family if there were better communication. Laura suggested that classes for parents on the Mega Center model would provide her with information she needed to understand the new thinking better. "I came to the sessions last summer," she said, "but now I could use more in-depth information."

Interactive Adult Decision Making. Through practice and continuing conversation, teachers and parents began to understand their new relationships, roles, and responsibilities. Planning for Mega Center's second year involved interactive decision making with parents. Suzanne Dawson designed a process in which teachers presented options on configurations of families of learners to parents at a Parent Teacher Organization meeting. Parents discussed the options and made suggestions. With a sigh of relief, one teacher reported how good she felt when, after considerable discussion, a parent said to the assembly, "We've given our input. Now let the educators handle this. They are the ones who have to work with the decisions next year."

Mega Center parents, teachers, and principal broke new ground in working together. The divergence of their metaphors on schooling for the children as well as conflicting metaphors on how parents involve themselves in school caused both pain and growth. Perhaps at first Mega Center teachers and administrators relied too heavily on the blind trust of the parents. Although the family-of-learners metaphor may have provided a reference point from which to develop Mega Center's close and explicit relationship with parents, other metaphors for parent involvement prevailed. This may indicate that including parents in the family of learners obscures rather than clarifies their role.

Plans for Mega Center's second year included initiating an on-site council. Representatives of parent and teacher groups and the principal would constitute the 13-member council. Authorized to make decisions ordinarily reserved for the district level, council members would have two-year terms. In laying the groundwork for the council at a faculty meeting near the end of the first year, Suzanne Dawson spoke of her hope that this organization would provide a vehicle for regular conversation on the nature of partnership between a school and the parents.

THE EARLY BABY

The architect of Mega Center, Paul Elson, designed the program "from scribbles on a piece of paper. . . . It was a dream come true," explained Paul, "to be given the opportunity to literally design this thing. But it's also frightening, you know, the fear of what if it doesn't work . . . and that's big-time fear." Paul reported that when he had arrived home the night the board approved Mega Center, his wife had said, "I bet you're thrilled." "No," Paul had responded, "I'm scared to death." Reflecting on the year, he added, "And if I had it to do over again, I think I would have worked harder with the teachers, the core staff, on how to deal with fear, because all of us dealt with fear all year long."

Not only was Paul called the architect of Mega Center, he also became known as its grandfather, godfather, or father. "Paul is the father of all this," commented one staff member. "This man parted waters for us. He's been working on this vision for a long time. . . . This is his child."

Family metaphors applied not only to Paul, but also to Mega Center itself. At a staff meeting early in the year, Suzanne Dawson referred to Mega Center as the "early baby." "Paul started with a vague idea," Suzanne said. "He didn't even know this school was going to come into existence when he began the design. This school wasn't supposed to be here right now—'91. This is the early baby."

In Paul's original plan, school year 1991–1992 would be a year for training interested school district teachers. At the end of the training, those interested would be given the opportunity to apply for positions. Because enrollment was growing on the city's east side, the district purchased a building and made plans to put 220 students in the building. The district's need for space forced Paul to present the Mega Center program to the board for approval and to begin implementation a year earlier than he intended. The budget, built on the assumption that there would be 220 students, was less than ideal for Mega Center. Suzanne believed that not being fully funded made Mega Center incredibly creative and interdependent. She saw no other meaning in the early-baby metaphor.

Paul's sense of fear provides clues to further understanding Mega Center as the early baby. Parents do fear for the life of their infants and hope for the healthy development of the early baby as Paul did for Mega Center. Paul was at Suzanne's side whenever there was a problem or crisis that threatened the vision. He both listened and gave advice and encouragement. Sometimes he chided the staff for back-sliding. He expressed fatherly pride in the Mega Center staff at their last meeting of the year. "I can honestly say you are absolute heroes of mine," said Paul. "I think you've done something that most people couldn't even think of doing and I salute you and congratulate you."

Mega Center was an early baby. Although the staff had six weeks of intensive training, the full year of training would have provided more time for reflection. Teachers would have had the opportunity to know one another as colleagues before engaging intensely in implementation challenges as members of teams. Some of the development that would have happened *in utero* during the preparation year occurred after Mega Center's birth.

FAMILY AND CULTURE

As Mega Center's culture developed during its first year, the family metaphor took root in the classrooms, where children interacted with their teachers and with other students. Children's identities became linked to being family members. For the adults, both teachers and parents, the family-of-learners metaphor did not take hold. Identity issues intermingled with boundary concerns, pushing against the family metaphor. Methods used in addressing schoolwide problems added to teachers' perceptions that Mega Center was developing a dysfunctional-family culture for the adults.

Identity

Mega Center's children began developing identities as members of particular families of learners even before school began. At an August open house students received visors whose color designated a particular family of learners, and the children wore them on the first day of school. Families had names, colors, slogans, and songs. The teachers warmly welcomed children into the families and discussed with them the expectations of members of their particular family and of the schoolwide family. Teachers exercised leadership in reducing the children's uncertainty and in helping them feel secure in their new school. Teachers took care to articulate the school-as-family metaphor whenever possible, embedding in the children's minds a way of thinking about their responsibilities and relationships at Mega Center.

Teachers at Mega Center worked diligently to provide a family atmosphere for the children. Many teachers described their role as being nurturers for the children. Nurturing encompassed not only giving children opportunities to grow in self-esteem but also providing an environment in which children could discover and delve into areas of particular interest. Mega Center's teachers were leaving behind the image of teacher as provider of knowledge and embracing the metaphor of teacher as nurturing adult, mentor, facilitator of learning, and lifelong learner. Teachers expressed growing comfort with this identity as they saw children engaging themselves in the learning process and giving evidence of their learning through performances and projects. Suzanne Dawson recognized and reinforced this new view of the role of teacher. A predominant cultural image of the Mega Center teacher became one of a nurturing adult.

Although Mega Center developed identity assumptions based on familial child-to-child and adult-to-child relationships, adults' relationships with one another were fraught with ambiguities. As a result, teachers and parents struggled to forge new identities that would form a basis for their new working relationships.

Amicable relationships usually resulted when teachers and parents met to discuss a child's progress. Participating in a parent-teacher conference was familiar professional ground for teachers. Most parents also had experience conferencing with teachers. Barring an unexpected confrontation, neither the teachers nor the parents had their identities at stake in these situations.

Parent involvement at Mega Center extended beyond activities such as conferences. As partners in their children's education, parents were expected to do their part in providing home learning environments and enrichment opportunities for their children. Teachers also hoped parents would volunteer to assist in classrooms, accompany groups on field trips, supervise in the Explore Room, and teach Travelogue classes. Even in these roles, parents would be working under the direction of the teachers. Although some activities would be new for parents, the identities of teachers and parents still derived from traditional teacher and parent metaphors.

Suzanne Dawson initiated structures through which parents took on the role of decision makers. Teachers felt threatened when they realized that parents saw themselves as responsible for providing enrichment opportunities for children in their families and for overseeing the curriculum. Faulty communication channels intensified teach-

ers' feelings of being discounted when they had no voice in some decisions they thought were theirs. As parent activity increased, teachers sensed a diminishment of their power and an invasion of their
boundaries. Parents, on the other hand, expressed frustration when
teachers did not implement the ideas and plans created by parent
groups. Although invited to be part of the creative educational process, they did not feel they were part of the Mega Center family, nor
did teachers know how to negotiate this role with the parents.

Identity issues also arose for teachers when they realized that if
they made certain decisions without consulting with their team members or if they revealed unpopular but strongly held beliefs, they risked
censure from their colleagues. They no longer had one-teacher/one-
classroom identities; instead, their professional identities were linked
with those of other members of their teams. Here, too, teachers perceived a curtailment of their professional power.

As Mega Center began its first year, both teachers and parents
dreamed of a school in which there would be permeable boundaries
and interactive decision making involving parents, teachers, principal, and sometimes children and the community. In the flurry of activity surrounding the opening of school, and in the days that followed,
day-to-day survival and crisis management became the norm. Attention to keeping the deeper promise of recasting teacher and parent
roles gave way to efforts to implement pledged programs.

Problem Solving

Mega Center's evolving patterns of schoolwide problem solving
provoked some teachers to describe the culture as that of a dysfunctional family. One teacher described dysfunction as not facing and
solving one's own problems. Even before school started, teachers
faced the challenge of addressing problem issues. In one instance, as
noted earlier, after the faculty had decided on names for their families, the strong dissenting voice of a person who had not been at the
meeting where the decision was made caused Suzanne Dawson to
reopen the issue. Teachers modified their original decision, but in
practice implemented the first decision. Strong dissenting voices influenced decisions at Mega Center. Verbal acquiescence to those decisions was important in order to be considered loyal to the vision of
the school. Teachers came to believe that expressing disagreement
would arouse more conflict than they could bear.

A second method of handling conflict employed by Suzanne
throughout the year was to call in an outside expert to resolve the
issue. The first incident involved a team of teachers assigned to space

that was not comparable to the space of the other families and that would not accommodate the number of children assigned to the family. Suzanne asked a person from the district office to assess the situation and give her a recommendation. The assessment coincided with the recommendation of the teachers involved, but Suzanne was not willing to make the decision without outside support. Despite Mega Center's attempts to cut a fresh path in education, reliance on the district office for advice became the norm.

A third problem-solving situation involved the Explore Room controversy. After listening to the administrative team, Suzanne summarized their recommendations. The option nobody raised involved revisiting the core problem of why there were not enough adults in the room to supervise the students. This discussion would have caused teachers to reexamine the preparation-time issue. Neither Suzanne nor the teachers were willing to face this head-on. Both principal and teachers gave tacit permission to avoid confronting difficult problems.

FAMILY AND JASON'S MAZE

Again, Jason's maze provides insight into a complex situation. Faced with a maze, a person assumes there is a way to proceed from beginning to end, however circuitous the path might be. Mega Center planners, teachers, and principal believed that including students, parents, educators, and the community in the family of learners would provide a pathway for them to travel together in their journey toward educational transformation. However, frequently they found themselves returning to the starting place—their former metaphors—to negotiate their way through the school year.

A second point of comparison deserves attention. Just as there are many paths through Jason's maze, many rich metaphors can provide ways to envision school life. As with all metaphors, the family metaphor reveals some, but not all, of the purposes of schooling. Additional metaphors of "school-as-firm, school-as-fair, and school-as-forum" could "sharpen a vision of excellence in schools" (Baker, 1991, p. 35). In forging their way through the maze of school reform, Mega Center's stakeholders would serve themselves well by going beyond the family-of-learners metaphor in areas where they meet blind alleys. Faced with this challenge, they could examine their experience and find new language to describe enhanced roles for parents and the community within the context of a school where teachers and students relate as family.

CHAPTER SEVEN

Teams

> One of the most promising proposals for school restructuring . . . involves redesigning the school's educational delivery system into teams made up of experienced, beginning, and apprentice teachers. . . . This team and a group of students, some replacing departing ones each year, would stay together for several years in a nongraded structure. (Goodlad, 1990, p. 301)

Although Mega Center's designers would not refer to its teams as "the school's educational delivery system," John Goodlad's description of team matches Mega Center's organization of teachers. Besides being a way to group teachers together for their work, team connotes a cooperative relationship. The nature of the cooperation draws its meaning from diverse metaphors.

TEAM AS METAPHOR

Although not germane to current use of the term, the word *team*, in its earliest definitions, has links to Mega Center's arrangement of students in families. Around the year 1000, *team* referred to childbearing and offspring, progeny, or family. The word also referred to and continues to mean a set of animals harnessed to draw together. Extending the meaning to persons drawing together, *team* took on the idea of persons associated in a joint action, especially persons forming a side in a sport. As early as the 1500s the meaning broadened to include a group collaborating in their professional work (OED, 1989).

An understanding of the purpose, content, and meaning of collaboration differed from person to person and from team to team for Mega Center's educators. Underlying some of their divergent ideas were not only conflicting metaphors for team but also ambiguities stemming from the shift in terminology from performance team to team.

One explanation of the diversity in metaphors for team derives from comparing how women and men describe the concept. For women, the idea of team incorporates the notion of community. Women emphasize cooperating to get work done, pitching in and doing whatever one can to help others, being responsible for the team result, and covering for somebody who slacks off (Harragan, 1982). They underscore the importance of supporting group action and achieving group satisfaction. "Women more often stress cooperation and collaboration whereas men tend to stress autonomy and individuality" (Shakeshaft, 1989, p. 207).

Men are more likely to describe a team player as a person who has a job to do and gets it done. For example, a ten-year-old boy will describe a team using baseball terminology in which

> there is nothing vague about that description, no generalized vagaries about "a bunch of guys supporting one another." By the time they are ten, little boys know . . . that a team is a very rigid structure and has a prescribed function, that each player covers his own position and nobody else's. (Harragan, 1982, p. 18)

Mega Center's plan called for its educators to move from being independent teachers to becoming interdependent team members. The contrast in these two modes of operation and the trial-and-error nature of the school's first year contributed to many teachers' expressions of uncertainty when talking about their roles as team members. The change involved a shift from private to public (Little, 1990). More than storytelling or lending assistance to other teachers, teaming requires considerable amounts of time and opens teachers' work to the scrutiny of others. Working as a team, teachers may experience praise, recognition, and support, or they may open themselves to criticism and conflict. For most, the contrast between the independence they had known in their former schools and the interdependence their joint work at Mega Center demanded required considerable adaptation. Although a few teachers described previous experiences of being team members in their schools, none of these experiences had the impact on their personal and professional lives that being a team member at Mega Center did.

Although the school's principal and most of the teachers were women, the teams struggled in attempting to work interdependently. When women or men professionally trained to be self-reliant find themselves under pressure or in ambiguous situations, they revert to their best-learned behaviors in order to be successful. Under stress, Mega Center teachers were no exception.

THE GENESIS OF TEAMS

Hired in June 1990, Mega Center teachers participated in six weeks of intensive orientation and training during the summer. A week-long August workshop was the reference point for both Suzanne Dawson and the teachers as they talked about teams. In May 1991, with the experience of almost a year behind her, Suzanne recalled feeling pressure from the teachers to decide who would be on each team during this training session.

"If I knew then what I know now, I think I would have stuck to my guns much harder when people were pushing to form teams," Suzanne reflected. At first Suzanne told teachers they could form planning teams, but these would not be the teams for their families. When they resisted her idea, she gave in and designed the teams that would work with each family of learners throughout the year. "We might have had a better schoolwide working spirit if I had held out," she continued, "because there would have been cross-energy." But this was Suzanne's first year as principal and, she reasoned, "coming from the role of a teacher I was too empathetic."

Suzanne Dawson's intuition told her to wait before forming teams, but, she admitted,

> I guess I didn't trust my intuition enough in those early days.
> . . . I wanted to empower the staff, and I let them do some deci-
> sion making without a lot of probing. At first I thought, "If
> that's what you want, that's what you get," instead of saying,
> "Let's look at this. What are the implications of this? What if we
> do it this way? These are the trade-offs. Is this really what you
> want?" Instead sometimes I said, "You make the decision and
> live with it." I think it would have been better if I had done a
> little more intervening in that process than I did.

Acquiescing to the teachers' pressure, Suzanne designated who would be on each team using a sociogram process. She asked teachers to write names of persons with whom they could work and the name of anyone with whom they might not be able to work. Based on teachers' preferences, Suzanne assembled five teams. Four teams included a kindergarten specialist, a special education certified teacher, and two elementary education certified teachers. Each team would work with one family of learners. In addition, Suzanne selected the resource team, a group of four teachers with art, music, physical education, science, and social studies expertise, to interact with all the families.

A teacher explained from her perspective the pressure teachers put on Suzanne to form teams:

> Energy was high during orientation, and we were all anxious to begin planning with our teams. We were excited about the new ideas we were learning on thematic instruction and wanted to get right into it. Besides, since we were sharing a room with another person, we were getting to know people quickly. We found ourselves telling each other things about ourselves that even our best friends didn't know. We became quite vulnerable to each other.

Only the experience of the first year would enable some teachers to see the process of choosing teams as a factor leading to Mega Center's becoming what some called "four schools within a school." "Staff cohesiveness? It doesn't exist. It doesn't exist," one teacher complained.

> First of all, teams were set up on a sociogram so everybody's working with who they perceived or thought were their friends. Many people who roomed together during orientation are on the same team. Well, if I'm working with my friends, who are all the other people? I chose the people I work with. That means I did not choose others. I think, in retrospect, that was a mistake.

Some new friendships suffered strain as teachers moved into teams together. Teachers expressed surprise and hurt when this happened. However, this phenomenon is not unusual, since enduring friendships among teachers usually remain at some distance from the classroom. Typically, "a school's staff may be described as 'close,' offering large doses of camaraderie, sympathy, and moral support, but the texture of collegial relations is woven principally of social and interpersonal interests" (Little, 1990, p. 513).

From the perspective of their professional lives, "quite apart from personal friendships or dispositions, teachers are motivated to participate with one another to the degree that they require each other's contribution in order to succeed in their own work" (Little, 1990, p. 520). When Mega Center teachers formed their teams, they did not realize the diversity of their beliefs and values. They had not yet had the opportunity to explore one another's professional strengths. They had not exchanged professional stories, nor had they given or received help from one another. Each wanted desperately to succeed. They wanted to make Mega Center a worldwide model of educational excellence. They thought that if they could begin planning together, they would be on the road to success. Mega Center's designers expected Suzanne and her staff to "hit the ground running." The teachers pressed to form teams before exploring their metaphors for teaming. Their beliefs and values revealed themselves as the teachers began working together. They began to see whether they had chosen as teammates the people they needed in order to succeed as Mega Center educators.

Behind the issue of team formation lurked an unaddressed question. Although Suzanne believed that problems arose among team members because she arranged teams too soon, later assignment to teams might not have alleviated future conflicts. Strong, conflicting ideas of what Mega Center would be and of how it would operate existed among teachers and between teachers and administration. Later arrangement of teams would not have solved this problem. The question of whether some individuals' images of the school would ever fit with the prevailing metaphors remained.

TEAM ISSUES

Teachers' views of the composition and purpose of teams surfaced in an early August interview session. Mega Center was hiring two teacher interns, graduate students at a local university who would be additional members of teams. In order to have a variety of teaching experiences, they would rotate among teams throughout the year. The six finalists met with Suzanne Dawson and three teachers. When asked if she had any questions, an interviewee inquired, "What is the greatest challenge for the teachers?" "Shall we start with survival!" Suzanne responded. One of the teachers, Mary Lee Kline, explained that many of the teachers were coming from traditional schools. "We have a word around here we call paradigm. The old paradigm is what we will want to go back to when things get hard." Another teacher, Bea Sheridan, continued, "This is where the team approach comes in. It will be so helpful. Teachers coming to Mega Center have been highly successful in the situations where they were. With the team, when things go poorly, people won't feel so bad. There will be other people to buoy a person up."

Mutual Support versus Task Orientation

Revealing their perspectives, Bea and Mary Lee exposed one of the three differences between the projection of *team* in Mega Center's plan and the reality of *team* in the school's implementation. These two teachers perceived a primary purpose of team as giving members mutual support. Their view is consistent with a feminine concept of team.

One of Mega Center's foundational documents described the function of team from another viewpoint. The document stated that the team would design learning experiences and projects for the families of learners after extensive consultation with parents. Although the teachers did not discount this function of team in their conversation, their first recognition, when faced with the magnitude of the task they were commencing, was the need for collegial support. On the other hand, congruent with masculine metaphors for team, Paul Elson had looked at the scope of the task and had delineated who would do it.

Team versus Performance Team

A second variation from the school's written plan involved dropping a word from the description of teams. Although Mega Center's design referred to the groups who would work with children as performance teams, teachers never used the word *performance* when speaking about teams. With their emphasis on mutual support and with the need for collegiality in planning, their descriptions of team conjured up images of working together within a small community. The notion of performance draws more heavily on images of team that Shakeshaft (1989) and Harragan (1982) refer to as masculine metaphors—that is, coordinating individual pieces to create a product.

Team Composition

A third difference between Mega Center's plan and its execution lay in the composition of the teams. Mega Center's blueprint listed teachers, a learning specialist, interns, aides, and volunteers as team members. When asked about challenges for teachers, Bea and Mary Lee immediately referred to teams as groups of teachers. The question of team composition remained a tacit issue throughout the year.

While teachers included the interns in team discussion and decision making as well as in teaching the children, volunteers assisted
teachers but did not share in decision making. Most aides saw themselves as working with students and teachers, but not with a team. At
the times when teams would meet, for example, before or after school,
during lunchtime, or while the children were in the Explore Room,
aides had assigned duties with the children. The structure of the day
excluded them from participation in team meetings during school time.
Since they received compensation only for their contact hours with
children, attendance at team meetings would have been on their own
time. However, even eliminating scheduling and compensation obstacles would have left the question of team composition unanswered.

At a January staff development meeting on conflict resolution, aides
related their concern about a lack of communication between themselves and the staff. When there is a problem, "aide goes to aide, aide
goes to another teacher, teacher goes to teacher, and the miscommu-
nication goes on," an aide commented. "Since we work closely with
children who have special needs, we should be involved in developing
their Individualized Educational Plans," another said. A teacher sided
with the aides' viewpoint. "I think teachers feel they are above aides,"
she remarked. The meeting facilitator added his perspective:

> This is an age of empowerment, and aides need empowerment
> by teachers. If you are a site-based-management model, aides
> are part of the family. What an aide has to say is as important as
> what the principal has to say. You are creating your own hier-
> archy. If you want Mega Center to be great, get rid of the hier-
> archy.

The facilitator's words reflected Mega Center's vision of including aides
as team members. However, since many teachers still labored to recognize their own power, even by the end of the year they had not
invited the voice of the aides into their conversation.

TEAMWORK

As Mega Center's teachers began working together, each team
developed its own norms and practices based on the teachers' beliefs
and experiences. Guidelines for team practice were scant. True to her
sense of empowering teachers, Suzanne Dawson expected each team
to develop its own format for working together.

Team Meetings

At a staff meeting Suzanne described team meetings as "opportunities to meet with your colleagues to brainstorm, to share, to confront if that's necessary, to do what's necessary so that you can provide quality education for the kids that come here."

In separate interviews, teachers working with the Elm family explained why they thought their team members functioned effectively together. "We respect each other," said one member; "we didn't put energy into team building, but we came with the same quality of life and a belief that we could make it work." Another member's perception was different. She believed the team "spent time on team development at the beginning of the year. We work well together," she observed; "we pass around leadership." The other two members echoed their colleagues' thoughts. "I love my team," one said; "our family is successful because we get along so well." "My peers here have been great," offered the other; "it's real satisfying to know that if I'm having a bad day I can talk to one of them. I'm not always looking for someone who agrees with me but someone who understands."

When the Elm family team members gathered for their hour-long weekly meeting on a Friday morning in January, they shared information on upcoming special events, sought advice from one another, and planned a field trip for their family of learners. Their conversation flowed easily from an item of business to a matter of personal concern to lighthearted humor.

An intern, Elaine Camden, commenting on her experience with the Elm family's team, explained how team members resolve issues involving conflict. "They just say we need to meet," she explained, "and that's good."

Elaine continued, contrasting this team with her first assigned team.

> In the other team I was with, if you said you needed to meet, people would ask why. . . . They thought if someone wanted to meet there was a problem. I wanted to meet so that we would feel a cohesiveness on the team. I felt like I was running around doing things by myself and then I'd say, "Oh, by the way, we did this change, we did that change," and yet I made the decisions on my own. Or else I'd talk to four different people in the hallway when I'd catch them and say, "Do you mind if we do this, do you mind if we do that." You know, it just didn't feel right. I was the facilitator and I didn't want that

position. I wanted us to work as a team, but if the team doesn't work together, if the team doesn't meet together enough, they just don't feel cohesive as a team. You can't just all of the sudden call a meeting and get five people together and present all the problems right then and there because it actually makes more problems and you lose ground before you gain any.

Compatible Values

The compatibility of values forms an essential basis for teachers to work together.

> Teachers' values are central to their self-image as people and as teachers, and are therefore the bedrock of their practice. So, they cannot work closely together with others who have different educational goals or views on how to achieve these, for to do so would create uncomfortable dissonance between their actions and their view of themselves. (Nias, 1989, p. 160)

Attempting to have people who are pursuing divergent objectives work together would be self-defeating because by definition they cannot pull together (Nias, 1989).

One Mega Center team hit the roadblock of incompatible values when they discovered that the kindergarten specialist was not sending children to the Explore Room. Instead she kept them in her classroom and gave them free play time. The specialist insisted the Explore Room was too confusing and chaotic for five-year-olds. "They are nurtured better in my room," she explained. Because the specialist needed to supervise children, she did not attend team meetings that had been scheduled for this time because all four teachers would be free of student responsibilities. Knowing one member would be absent from meetings, other team members met infrequently. Incompatible values led to diverse choices that continued to pull this team apart throughout the year.

From Independence to Interdependence

Moving from being an independent teacher to an interdependent team member posed challenges for Mega Center's teachers. Some teams struggled in trying to understand their purpose and function. Mega Center's teachers had experienced success in their former schools. Operating independently, they had developed original ideas and effective strategies for engaging children in learning. They came to Mega Center hoping to find an environment where collegiality was the norm. But Mega Center was not a ready-made environment. One teacher divulged her shock when, faced with a dilemma, she realized, "The greatest resource at my fingertips was me!" Teachers would not find an environment in their new magnet school; they would create it.

When faced with divergent views or conflict, some team members withdrew physically or emotionally from participation in the team and "went solo," causing tension and misunderstanding. They would "get the job done," while reverting to being autonomous teachers. "This is the only way we know how to survive," commented one teacher.

More than any other single issue, teachers talked of their need to develop as team members. One teacher explained,

> We've never had one in-service on what teaming is or how to do it effectively. Now we're having a consultant come in and do conflict resolution. But if we were set up, equipped to team better, maybe we wouldn't be spending a day finding out how to resolve conflicts.

Another teacher commented,

> One of the biggest problems that faced this school—they didn't foresee it and they are still facing it—is how to build teams. . . . What has to be defined is what people are expected to do as team members. . . . Certain people are being allowed to pull back and be autonomous and not be team players and not support the team system and not support the school.

"I'm hazy on how teaming works," commented a veteran teacher. Another teacher said, "Teaming is difficult. Their concept of teaming is not real clear if they haven't done it. . . . It has to come from the top down." Teachers preferred that the administration establish team norms rather than establishing the norms themselves.

IMAGES OF TEAM

Mega Center teachers faced a plethora of issues as they worked together as team members. Underlying the daily dilemma of being team members were questions about whether this arrangement would enhance the professional practice of teachers and lead to excellent education for children. As competing metaphors and divergent practices surfaced during the year, teachers began to realize their need to explore how their understanding of team was linked to Mega Center's success.

Sports Metaphor

Team as a sports metaphor found its way into Mega Center's thinking. When teachers focused on "getting the job done," they employed a sports image. The school's vision emphasized cooperating with others and competing only with oneself. However, teachers did compare themselves with others, wondering, for example, why someone else's room looked cleaner or more interestingly decorated than theirs, or speculating on how some families of learners could go on more expensive field trips than others.

Two instances of using sports metaphors occurred in reference to the principal. A teacher said she had hoped Suzanne would be more of a coach for teachers because she was a marvelous teacher herself. Several parents referred to Suzanne as an excellent cheerleader for the vision of the school. "She is articulate and enthusiastic," explained one parent, "and she keeps putting the vision out there."

Each week at the head of her newsletter for teachers and staff members, Suzanne Dawson placed a quotation, which she later described as a reflection of her own thinking, similar to what one might write in a journal. In four of the first eight weeks of the year, the quotations came from persons in the sports world—three coaches and one Olympic gold medalist.

Ecological Images

Suzanne introduced a video entitled *Teamwork* at a faculty meeting in early January by saying, "Paul Elson wanted you to see this." In less than three minutes teachers viewed nature scenes, trees, deer, waterfalls, lakes, many from a top-down perspective, and heard a soothing feminine voice narrate:

> Teamwork flourishes when members communicate feelings and resolve conflict. . . . What is a trusting relationship? According to one writer it is the knowledge that you will not deliberately or accidentally, consciously or unconsciously, take unfair advantage of me. It means that I can put my situation at the moment, my status and my self-esteem in this group, our relationship, my job, my career, even my life in your

hands with complete confidence. The best teams are also clear on their goals and how each person contributes to reaching them. . . . There is something special that happens when people work well together, a synergy that multiplies effort, that enhances contributions and brings out the best in each of us. (Tager, 1990)

With this video, Paul and Suzanne offered visual and verbal pictures of what teamwork should look like. But Suzanne did not provide time for discussion of the video. The images served not to soothe but to frustrate some teachers. They too experienced disappointment in their efforts at teamwork. They needed time to develop trust and guidance to articulate images of what their teams would look like. They needed to step aside from their professional habit of going directly from problem to solution and reflectively paint their own alternative scenarios of teamwork.

Schools Within a School

While acknowledging the individuality of students and teachers, some teachers and parents disparagingly referred to Mega Center as "four schools within a school." They expected teams to develop similar practices and provide similar experiences for the students. Often it was not enough for Suzanne to explain how the school's thematic curriculum tied instruction together among the families of learners and the teams. Each team needed time and privacy in which to develop working relationships and "interactive professionalism," Michael Fullan's (1991) term describing team functioning. Fullan sees teams as "teachers and others working in small groups interacting frequently in the course of planning, testing new ideas, attempting to solve different problems, assessing effectiveness, etc." (p. 142). In this setting teachers would give and receive advice openly and confidently. They would be "continuous learners in a community of interactive professionals" (p. 142).

Following on this theory, teachers who imagined their roles as interactive professionals would have the knowledge and confidence needed to support four schools within a school. Relying on more than interpersonal relationships, the professional expertise they brought with them to Mega Center could not only enhance their practice but also renew their self-esteem. Being "continuous learners in a community of interactive professionals" brings purpose and function to the concept of team.

A Competing Image

Although images of team pervaded the thinking of Mega Center's teachers, the image of an eagle became the symbol for individual adults. The name arose when, at a summer meeting, Paul Elson remarked, "There are no ducks here; you're all eagles." Suzanne picked up on the metaphor, institutionalizing it by naming the weekly faculty and staff bulletin *Eagle Notes*.

David McNally's *Even Eagles Need a Push* (1990) became a reference book for Suzanne. A quotation from the book in the October 15 *Eagle Notes* read, "We can learn to soar only in direct proportion to our determination to rise above the doubt and transcend the limitations" (p. 11). Suzanne established a reserved parking spot near the door for the "Eagle of the Week," the teacher or aide whose picture and brief biography hung on a bulletin board near the office each week.

Teachers never referred to themselves as eagles, although one teacher used the title "head eagle" for Suzanne. After discussing a situation in which the teacher described the children's behavior as "way out of line," she asked Suzanne to intervene. "It's head eagle time," she said. Suzanne replied, "With claws, huh?"

Suzanne used the term *eagle* both to praise and to chide teachers and other personnel. When a new maintenance engineer came to Mega Center in October, she told the teachers, "I want you to know the insider stuff on George. . . . I hope all you eagles will swoop down on him and let him know he's found his nest. Those already working with him know he is the essence of an eagle." Another time Suzanne said, "You have come to depend on *Eagle Notes* to tell you when you have duty. But guess what? You're eagles, and eagles fly on their own."

The choice of *eagles* and *teams* as descriptors for Mega Center's teachers placed contradictory metaphors on them and teachers seemed to sense this in their reluctance to adopt the term *eagle*. The individual character of the eagle and the group orientation of the team provided competing images and caused confusion for teachers in how they should think about their roles. The paradox in the images disregarded the power of language to shape practice and contributed to ongoing tensions.

Although the eagle metaphor became a familiar one, teachers tried focusing on teams rather than on solo flights. Most of the teachers had experienced individual successes and now became absorbed in another aspect of professional development, becoming a team member. "This is why we came here," remarked one teacher.

TEAM AND CULTURE

Mega Center teachers faced challenging issues as they approached the task of educational reform. Developing a collegial culture where teamwork was the norm would be laden with difficulties. At stake were questions of identity and power.

Identity

Mega Center teachers came from schools where parents, administrators, and colleagues recognized them as excellent educators. At their new school individual success was related to team effectiveness. Even when teachers provided creative learning opportunities for students, if teams were treading water or submerged in conflict, teachers tended to view themselves as unsuccessful. Although they were chosen for this school because of their competency and creativity, teachers began to doubt themselves as effective educators because they could not adapt readily to the new role of interdependent team members.

From Paul Elson's perspective, team building was a six-step process of moving from independent to collaborative work. The movement would take place over time and would involve critical transition periods in which teams could revert to previous behaviors or move closer to collaboration. The difference between Paul's perspective and the teachers' perceptions lay in their expectation that they would be interdependent and collaborative from the beginning.

Teachers wanted to live up to Suzanne's expectation that they would "hit the ground running." Even in its first days of operation, the school was open to visitors, leaving little privacy for teachers to learn by trial and error. Teachers lived with the fear of being criticized by observers or by school personnel who accompanied observers. Despite Suzanne's words that mistakes would be opportunities for improvement, a growing cultural assumption was that there would not be room for error at Mega Center.

Teachers became discouraged when they experienced dissonance between their expectations and their experience. Overwhelmed with work, many found it easier to plan alone whenever possible than to collaborate with others. Yet some teachers were willing to spend time and energy on team building. They had seen glimpses of the personal and professional benefits of teamwork.

For most Mega Center teachers, working as interactive teams required more than planning, generating and testing new ideas, solving problems, and evaluating effectiveness. In addition to being trusted as capable professionals, they expressed the need to rely on one another for personal support that would sustain their professional efforts. They hoped teaming would provide opportunities for discussing professional successes and failures and for sharing personal ups and downs. Unable to slough off personal criticism, they needed a culture in which they would be individually esteemed and professionally respected. Yet, as the year wore on, conflicts among individuals escalated, causing Suzanne to call in district personnel to mediate situations.

Teachers did not see their personal and professional lives as separate entities. Instead, they perceived their professional lives as closely connected to their home lives. Being in teams put them into relational settings in which they needed to respect one another's ways of being human as well as to understand one another's ways of being teachers. But continually they found themselves floundering in their attempts to get along and to form cohesive teams.

Mega Center's founders expected teams to involve not only teachers but also aides, parents, and other support staff. Teamwork would center around planning educational experiences for children. The stresses of being in the public eye and the feelings of loss of identity as a teacher were so great that Mega Center teachers needed not only to establish personal trust in one another but also to receive individual reassurance and support from their principal before they could become interdependent team members. Only when they struggled with their own self-esteem and identity issues could Mega Center teachers give energy to developing teams that would become interactive professional communities of persons who would give one another personal respect and support.

Power

The closely connected issues of power and boundaries impinged on Mega Center's efforts to create a collaborative culture. Although quick to criticize hierarchical structures that limited their participation in decision making, teachers maintained arrangements that prevented others from joining them as team members. Interns were considered part of teams; aides were not. Initial plans also included volunteers as team members, but they were never invited to participate in team meetings. Although in theory teachers were attempting to break down barriers to communication and to develop interactive decision making, they reserved most professional discussions and decisions for themselves.

When faced with the issue of including aides in teams at the January conflict-resolution seminar, most teachers remained quiet. As noted earlier, the seminar leader told them that Mega Center would be an excellent school when it got rid of its hierarchy and the aide's voice held as much weight as the principal's voice. But the teachers themselves had not experienced the power of their voices, so they remained silent.

Suzanne gave teachers the authority to implement schoolwide decisions in whatever ways they thought best. She encouraged them to be innovative in creating learning experiences for their students. She urged them to develop the model of team that would work best for them as individuals. Yet teachers did not feel empowered because they had no voice in other critical decisions that affected their lives, such as moving a child from one family to another. Nor did they have opportunities to discuss whether to implement various components of Mega Center's program, for example, beginning theaters of learning. Feeling disenfranchised themselves, they were not ready to open up their teamwork to others.

Throughout the year Suzanne did what she could to assist teams when they experienced trouble. Although she urged teachers to solve problems among themselves, she would intervene when requested. When situations seemed irreconcilable, she transferred teachers from one team to another. Suzanne and the teachers knew they needed to realign team members for the following year since the school would have to accommodate nine-year-olds. They hoped these personnel changes would alleviate some problems. But unless both Suzanne and the teachers addressed the identity and power issues, realignment would only mask the problems inherent in Mega Center's culture.

TEAM AND JASON'S MAZE

Like finding a path through a maze, the process of team building was a trial-and-error experience for most Mega Center teachers. Faced with unexpected blockages and difficult-to-negotiate circumstances, team members expressed the feeling that often they were back to square one, the beginning of the maze. Some teachers needed a new maze, a reconfigured team, before they could begin to find their way. Others moved more slowly through the maze, mediating difficulties and conflicts before they became dead ends.

Just as there were many paths through Jason's maze, Mega Center teachers faced the challenge of understanding themselves and their work from several new perspectives. They would be educators rather than teachers, team members rather than independent teachers. In addition to being "interactive professionals," they would be adult family members and members of a community of learning. Teachers needed time to work their way through this maze of identities. Signing on at Mega Center, they knew they had committed themselves to change, but they did not know how deep and complex the change would be, nor did they realize how easy it would be to get lost in the maze.

Although the team approach reflected the school's planners' belief that children benefit from cooperation and collaboration of adults, in practice, Mega Center's teams faltered for several reasons. Moving from the familiar role of independent teacher to the new identity of interdependent team member required significant adaptation for teachers. The notion of team itself evoked diverse metaphors with contrasting masculine and feminine perspectives and with differing expectations of team members. Conflicting ideas on what Mega Center should be and what the school should do presented obstacles to team efforts. Finally, the paradox of the competing eagle and team metaphors added confusion rather than clarity to team practice.

The arrangement of Mega Center's teachers into teams was more than a component of the school's program. Teams would enable Mega Center to provide educational experiences for children in ways not possible in one-teacher/one-classroom configurations. Teams were at the core of Mega Center's infrastructure. Mega Center's efforts at reforming education would be successful only when productive teamwork happened.

CHAPTER EIGHT

Vision-Keeper

On the last day of school, when Mega Center's principal, Suzanne Dawson, heard the story of Jason's maze, she smiled, sighed, and quietly repeated Jason's words, "There are really lots of ways to do it." Her response revealed her recognition of the maze as a poignant image of Mega Center's startup year and of her first year as principal. Mega Center's designers wanted a principal with no previous experience, someone who had never been through the maze. They hoped she would cut a fresh leadership path through the maze of the school's first year. They anticipated that with her leadership, teachers would commit themselves to the vision and to its implementation. Teachers envisioned open communication, shared power, and joint decision making as normative.

The district superintendent selected Suzanne as principal because she was an experienced and innovative educator, a certified administrator, and a recognized leader among her peers. For several years her mentor had urged her to become a school principal, but Suzanne had resisted. Explaining the circumstances that brought her to Mega Center's principalship, she revealed,

> There are no accidents. The timing was perfect. I had just fin-
> ished my doctoral work, and the district was opening this
> school. I was given the vision, not a blank slate. It was such a
> perfect match. I could agree with everything in the vision and I
> was excited.

VISION-KEEPER AS METAPHOR

From early on, vision-keeper became Suzanne's metaphor for her leadership role. She believed she was responsible for holding the vision high so its light would illuminate the path through the maze of the year. From time to time, more frequently than she had expected, she found herself running into blocked pathways and following circuitous routes. The maze of the principalship and the maze of the year were more complex than she had imagined.

Traditional View of Leaders

Although Mega Center's principal and teachers considered the expression *vision-keeper* uniquely theirs, the metaphor finds its roots in leadership literature. Peter Senge (1990) describes the differences between the traditional view of leaders and a new view of leadership. The traditional view, rooted in an individualistic and nonsystemic view of the world, sees leaders as

> special people who set the direction, make key decisions, and energize the troops. . . . At its heart, the traditional view of leadership is based on assumptions of people's powerlessness, their lack of personal vision and inability to master the forces of change, deficits which can be remedied only by a few great leaders. (p. 340)

Based on a school-as-organization model, the vision-keeper metaphor assumes there is an official set of beliefs that the leader guards. The leader is responsible for protecting the institutional vision and is accountable to superiors for the success of the implementation. With the vision-keeper metaphor, "there is still an expectation that particular leadership tasks can be ascribed to a hierarchical position and that these will be instrumental in the realization of organizational goals" (Angus, 1989, p. 75). The magnitude of the tasks sets the vision-keeper apart from and above the implementors. Despite its contemporary ring, the vision-keeper metaphor draws its meaning from traditional notions of leadership.

Leaders in Learning Communities

In contrast with the traditional view, Senge (1990) calls leaders designers, stewards, and teachers, responsible for building learning communities "where people continually expand their capabilities to understand complexity, clarify vision, and improve shared mental models" (p. 340).

Most often principals and teachers find themselves entrenched in traditional views of hierarchical leadership. However, if leadership is to contribute to educational reform that goes beyond offering more of the same in disguise, it will be necessary to conceive of school leadership as something other than part of a top-down hierarchy. Leaders are not necessarily those in "positions of leadership," and people may exercise leadership or perform an act of leadership on some occasions but not on others. (Angus, 1989, p. 86)

Building a learning community based on principles of mutuality and shared responsibility offers a challenge to educators trained and practiced in top-down models of leadership and followership.

BUILDING A SHARED VISION

Despite efforts to break through traditional hierarchical notions of principalship, Suzanne Dawson's image of principal as vision-keeper constrained her from engaging in processes of building a shared vision, especially early in the school year. The school's designers had handed her a ready-made vision, and Suzanne guarded it closely. In contrast, building shared vision is a continuous, never-ending role of leaders.

For those in leadership positions, what is most important to remember is that their visions are still personal visions. Just because they occupy a position of leadership does not mean that their personal visions are *automatically* "the organization's vision." (Senge, 1990, p. 214)

As described in Chapter 5, at a fall faculty meeting Suzanne Dawson enlisted the help of the district consultant Paul Elson to articulate the school's vision in the light of growing personnel problems. Paul described Mega Center as a magnificent idea and warned teachers not to get in the way of the idea, lest it fail. Emphasizing the importance of shared vision, he urged them to resolve their conflicts. Senge (1990) gives a different perspective on the relationship between an idea and a shared vision. He argues that

shared vision is not an idea. . . . It may be inspired by an idea, but once it goes further—if it is compelling enough to acquire the support of more than one person—then it is no longer an abstraction. It is palpable. People begin to see it as if it exists. Few, if any, forces in human affairs are as powerful as shared vision. (p. 206)

Throughout the year Suzanne struggled, trying to make sense of the impasse of keeping the vision, mediating staff conflict, and empowering the faculty to share and to shape the vision.

Suzanne's education and professional experience had taught her that principalship involved assuming diverse roles. As vision-keeper she saw herself as change agent. In this position she would be shaping the very culture of the school. From the perspective of the school as an organization, she would have to be involved in both the leadership and the management of the school. A study of the urban high school documents the importance of both leadership abilities and sophisticated management skills in schools involved in the change process (Louis & Miles, 1990). Thomas Sergiovanni (1992b) affirms that both organization and community metaphors reveal certain aspects of school life. "But," he claims, "it makes a world of difference which of the two provides the overarching frame" (p. 41). Suzanne found herself in the paradoxical position of being vision-keeper, leader, and manager while at the same time seeing the school as a family and trying to include the voices of parents, children, and teachers in the family conversation. The metaphorical discrepancies led to practical tensions. Throughout the year Suzanne searched for ways to reconceptualize her vision of leadership.

KEEPING THE FAMILY VISION

Central to Mega Center's vision is the family-of-learners metaphor. Providing a safe and secure environment, building self-esteem, and teaching interpersonal skills originate in the family metaphor. When the leader internalizes the school's primary metaphor, the image informs the person's practice. Suzanne Dawson's daily interactions with children revealed her deep understanding of the centerpiece of Mega Center's vision.

Teacher after teacher praised what one teacher called "Suzanne's incredible dedication, caring, and sensitivity to the vision. She wants what's best for kids, and that's the best part." Suzanne treated the children with personal attention and warmth. "Dr. Dawson, my mom had a baby girl," a shy six-year-old whispered in Suzanne's ear on the way in to school one morning. Suzanne congratulated the child, hugged her, and sent her on, urging her to tell the good news to the whole Elm family.

Often on their birthdays children visited Suzanne's office, sometimes with a treat for her, and sometimes just to tell her it was their special day. Suzanne would drop everything, wish them happy birthday, and have conversations about how special they were.

Each Tuesday the children in one home base had lunch with the principal in the parent lounge. Suzanne arranged the tables with special tablecloths and centerpieces. She provided dessert for the children and visited with the entire group, then with each individual child.

Occasionally behavior problems brought a child to Suzanne's office. Gently but firmly, Suzanne guided the child to acknowledge wrongdoings and to determine how to make amends. A few children periodically came to Suzanne's office to discuss what they might do when they thought they might be headed toward conflict with another child. To Suzanne, these children were family. She knew each by name and generously offered them encouragement for their efforts and praise for their good work.

VISIONS OF LEADERSHIP

Personal Beliefs

The leader's personal beliefs and values influence the vision of a school. Although the leader's vision remains an individual vision until it coalesces with the visions of others to form a shared vision, the leader's metaphors carry power by virtue of the leadership position. When a school engages in reform efforts, the principal's vision, with its metaphors, is key in shaping the culture and implementing the change. Knowledge of the leader's personal beliefs about schooling assists in understanding the person's interpretation of the vision.

Mega Center's principal, Suzanne Dawson, drew meaning for her work as an educational leader from her own love of learning. "I think that's one thing that has been both a curse and a blessing in my life," she explained. "I'm never satisfied. But then, that's also, I think, what kept me alive—keeps me alive." Her role model was her grandmother, who died at the age of 99.

It was very, very hard to get her to talk about the past because she was too interested in the present and in the future. She couldn't get enough new. She was fascinated by news. Her eyesight was so bad that she couldn't read herself, so she had people reading two and three newspapers a day to her. And she listened to news. She loved Cable Network News because it was on 24 hours a day. And she would discuss it. It wasn't enough that she took all this in; she would formulate ideas about it and always be interested in talking about what was happening in the world. And at 99 when you are so frail that you can't get out of bed, why should you be interested in the future and what's going on in the world when your whole world is confined to bed? But hers wasn't because her mind was her world instead of her environment.

Suzanne continued, relating her experience with her grandmother to her vision of education for children:

And so to create in children that kind of belief and motivation to make their minds their world . . . we do that a little bit with reading, magic reading—get into a book and you can fly anywhere and be anywhere in the world. We do that for kids. But we stop there. And part of what I think the mission of educators is, is to create that kind of intellectual hunger and curiosity and delight—a delight in learning—so that it never stops no matter what they do. . . . To me if we can do that for children, we can affect the world.

Describing her vision of schooling, Suzanne explained,

My whole theory is that every school, every grade, every classroom should look like a well-run kindergarten—at the appropriate developmental level. When you stop to think about how kindergartens work, how really good kindergartens work, there are times when the whole group comes together, there are times when the children go to centers to explore and to create. . . . Based on their own internal interests and their own internal motivation, they build naturally on the knowledge they have. That seems to me to translate very, very naturally into an approach to learning. As kids learn more, they have questions, they want to find more answers, they do more exploring.

Referring to Howard Gardner's (1985) multiple intelligences, Suzanne continued:

Traditional schools emphasize logical mathematical and linguistic intelligences. And yes, schools do teach music, they teach physical education, they teach art, but they teach them as separate entities. They don't teach them as personal extensions of an individual. They're kind of external entities imposed on top of who you are. . . . So instead of approaching education from an externally imposed set of things, starting with the child first and moving out—it's the most difficult thing for teachers to deal with because they've been trained to be the great sage on the stage. . . . And Mega Center isn't close to adopting this perspective.

Reflecting further on Mega Center's first year, Suzanne said,

I think that's such a delicate balance, and it's a balance that we haven't found yet. I don't think we're there, but that's something that I see as an important mission for the school—to find when does the structure enable and when does the structure inhibit. I think at Mega Center we've been on a pendulum swing. In some cases we just impose the structure, and in other cases there's not enough. . . . I think children need enough structure to guide their thinking and to stimulate them. They need to be asked the right questions to develop that whole cycle of curiosity and exploration. And I see that as a major goal for us to discover.

Discussing another aspect of her beliefs about Mega Center, Suzanne commented, "I think the main philosophical theory behind Mega Center is that children need to learn from a lot of different sources, in a lot of different ways, and some children will learn at one time and others will learn at another." Suzanne paused, laughed, and commented parenthetically, "You know, I think adults are really less in charge of that than we'd like to be."

Comparing Mega Center with other schools in the district, Suzanne said,

The other magnets provide choices in terms of an emphasis, but most do not use alternative methods of delivering instruction. . . . Mega Center needs to move in a direction where children really do have a voice in how they learn and what they do. . . . Not that they determine the curriculum, I mean, it's not totally choice. . . . But within the context of curriculum, or within the context of a group theme and group experiences, children need to have opportunities both to explore and to choose where they want to function.

Suzanne Dawson wanted Mega Center to be exciting and challenging, a place children loved coming to. She wanted teachers to be free from constraints, able to use their ingenuity to provide a safe, nurturing school environment and creative, integrated learning experiences for children. She wanted to build a culture in the school in which decisions centered on children's needs and the entire staff listened to the voices of children and their parents.

The school's mission statement reflected the vision Suzanne had accepted. She wanted the children, parents, educators, and community members to work together as a family of learners to foster an enthusiasm for lifelong learning. Convinced that successful implementation of the vision, with its embedded metaphors, would make Mega Center an exemplary institution, Suzanne exerted unbounded energy monitoring and safeguarding the vision.

Suzanne explained how her work at Mega Center brought meaning to her life.

> I want to make a difference in the world. . . . I talk about writing articles, and I want to do that not because I want to collect things under my bibliography but because I want to share what I find with other people. So a large part of my vision is creating something that can be given away, not only to the children that we have here, but to anybody who comes into that building and who wants to know about it. And when you stop to think how, as teachers, we touch lives and have the power, the immense power, to impact lives and that those lives go on and on, it's incredible power. . . . Education is one field that has the most potential for creating a world of beauty and harmony and love and caring that extends across international boundaries and that's a tremendous responsibility, but that doesn't happen naturally. And we have to do it. . . . I can be a vision-keeper. I can be a vision-exposer, maybe. I can help other people build their visions and their dreams, but I guess I don't dream small dreams. Mega Center is only a small piece of the big puzzle which is the world. If we just do it at Mega Center that's nice, but that's not enough. . . . Think of the power when we stop thinking internally and begin to think externally. And in education I don't think we've done enough of that. . . . We tend to think my classroom is what I have to affect. My school system is what I have to affect. The world is what I have to affect! When you start thinking "What have I got that I can give away?" there's a whole different mind set. It isn't competitive any more and everybody gets the best of everybody else's work to do with it what they can.

Although Suzanne embraced her beliefs with conviction, she felt buffeted with doubts in the face of criticism:

> When you call your beliefs into question, you challenge a very fundamental part of who you are, which is a real earthshaking kind of confrontation, a personal confrontation. And add to that a lot of stress and strain with people questioning you, especially parents asking, "Are you doing this right? Is my kid learning?" and you say to yourself, "Whoa! I don't know!" That gets to be real, real unnerving.

As a first-year principal, Suzanne felt strong pressure to implement Mega Center's vision. She did not want to disappoint the district superintendent, who appointed her principal; Frances Mayer and the school board, who approved the implementation of the project; and Paul Elson, who designed the plan for the school. Suzanne measured Mega Center's progress against the beliefs and values that shaped her vision. When parents or teachers challenged programs or practices, Suzanne felt personally vulnerable. She saw herself as the primary spokesperson for and keeper of Mega Center's vision.

Vision-Keeping

Seeing the Big Picture. When Suzanne Dawson talked about her role as principal, invariably she mentioned Mega Center's vision. Although she disliked being directive, she found there were times when she thought the vision required it.

> You listen to the input and respect that input because the teachers know what they are talking about. But ultimately when I make a decision it's always measured against the philosophy, always measured against the vision. . . . Somebody's always got to keep the big picture in mind. You can get lost in the everyday stuff. Everyday stuff has to get done, but you can't get lost in it. And you've got to be able to stand back and look at the big picture and say, "What's happening here?"

Suzanne used written communications as a primary means to keep the vision in front of parents and teachers. The parent newsletter contained articles on Mega Center's vision and programs. The staff's weekly bulletin, *Eagle Notes*, included affirmations and quotations pertaining to the vision.

Teachers had mixed reactions to the affirmations, quotations, and other vision-oriented suggestions in the bulletin. Some said they felt insulted that Suzanne would think they needed reminders about what they thought they were already doing; others appreciated the encouragement they read in the statements. Some saw the affirmations as laying down behavioral norms requiring them to "think happy" or "be positive." They saw the vision orientation as a way to avoid facing recurring problems. Other teachers expressed relief at having a principal who trusted their instructional decisions but wanted personal reassurance that they were implementing the vision. Some tried to hide their discouragement and insecurity from the vision-keeper.

Guarding or Sharing the Vision. Both Suzanne and the teachers felt the tension of the contradiction between guarding an imposed vision and building a shared vision, but they were not conscious of the source of the dilemma. Vision-keeping demands control; vision-sharing necessitates flexibility. Suzanne's natural orientation as a leader moved toward flexibility, but the vision-keeper metaphor required control. Building a shared vision would require time, trust, and release from the constraints of an imposed vision. It would also require Suzanne to shift from thinking of herself as vision-keeper to finding a new leadership metaphor.

A teacher described Suzanne as leading with her energy. Suzanne used the phrase "cast in shifting sands" to describe her own flexibility. She had a high tolerance for ambiguity and saw Mega Center as constantly evolving. "Part of the vision," she explained, "is not to ever be complete. Part of the vision is to always be searching for something new, to always be looking at what research is telling us."

Suzanne's predominant mode of engaging teachers in the vision was to turn over to them, individually or as teams, responsibility for implementation. For example, she gave each teacher a copy of curriculum recommendations of the National Council of Teachers of Mathematics (NCTM), expecting that teachers would develop their curriculum based on the recommendations. "I've been reading NCTM's stuff for the last four or five years," she said. "They've said throw out the textbooks, you've got calculators, teach kids estimation, teach kids problem solving, forget the worksheets, forget the traditional story problems. Make it real." Suzanne continued, "And educators and textbook writers have been plugging their ears and looking [in] the other direction. And nobody has really had the courage to take that leap of faith."

Referring to Mega Center's mission of being an example of school transformation, Suzanne said,

I really hope we can hold to creating our own math curriculum. We are finding there are good things for primary age children, but there's nothing for intermediate, so you go back to the old paradigm. It is my hope that Mega Center can be the school that takes those ideas from those experts, and puts them into a practical setting, and tries them, and refines them, and builds curriculum, and builds models. Then we could share them with other educators . . . that's my hope. And my fear is that when we're trying, we'll find some things that work, and work really well, and hunker down, and put them into place, and as others put them in place, we'll begin to look a lot like everyone else. They will have followed us but we won't be at the cutting edge any more. That's my fear. But that won't happen as long as I'm here.

Suzanne had an intuitive grasp of how each teacher's contribution fit into the building of the vision. For example, she pointed to one teacher's leadership in developing a community-service component in the school. Working with the student council, the teacher developed a schoolwide recycling program. Suzanne believed the community-service part of the vision would continue to evolve and become a significant aspect of Mega Center's life.

Suzanne's view of herself as vision-keeper put her in the position of funneling information to and from individual teachers, teams, and the entire faculty. The tight coupling between Suzanne and the vision prevented some teachers from voicing their views. Some said they were not certain that their voices mattered. Others expressed concern about communication channels, stating that the information flow in the school was not balanced. Other teachers, consumed by the challenges and time requirements of implementing the vision or discouraged by inconsistencies they perceived between the vision and practice, chose to focus their energies on working with the children. Suzanne did not see that her role as vision-keeper informed, and sometimes impeded, her work with the teachers.

Being vision-keeper provided Suzanne with motivation and satisfaction.

That's the joy for me. To be the vision-keeper, first of all you have to have the vision. And the vision is always forward. The vision is always the best and never a vision of what's negative. It's a vision of what you're striving for in its purest form. And keeping that vision, finding the vision, having the vision evolve, because it changes for me based on circumstances, is what gets me up in the morning.

Suzanne's vision, like any leader's vision, reflected a personal and unique viewpoint. Just as it is difficult to describe an image captured by the human eye, it is challenging to clearly articulate beliefs and values. Because perspective affects what each person sees, sharing a vision involves inherent problems. The notion of vision as a metaphor for the beliefs and values of an institution contributes to the difficulty of bringing about institutional agreement because of the individual character of vision. Caught in the confusion of personal, imposed, and shared visions, Mega Center's principal and teachers avoided the issue by concentrating on making the school good for the children.

Leaderless Leadership

Reflecting on the year, Suzanne described herself as being in the process of growing. She said she had gained new insights into education and new insights into people through both good and bad experiences. "But," she admitted, "I'm still not comfortable with assuming the leadership role."

Suzanne's discomfort with leadership stemmed, in part, from the tension between her natural intuitive, energetic, and forward-looking style along with her sense of herself as vision-keeper, and her sincere desire to empower the teachers and parents to work together to implement the vision while trying to please and placate everyone. She talked more frequently about people "having the vision" than about "sharing the vision." Occasionally at faculty meetings she gave pep talks on "not settling for being pretty-darn-good, but striving for excellence." On several occasions she found herself in situations both with parents and with teachers where she became defender of the vision.

Although Suzanne encountered questions and even opposition, she did not seem to realize fully that her vision was one among many visions held by Mega Center teachers and parents. For Mega Center to thrive, Suzanne needed to enable teachers to articulate and clarify Mega Center's overarching metaphor. If Mega Center, at its core, were to become a family of learners, as its foundational documents indicated, the adult family members had to engage in dialogue about what bonded them as family. They had to work toward developing a shared vision. They had begun this discussion in August and presumed it was completed. But the experience of the year demonstrated that they had only begun the process of developing a shared vision.

Defining the Role. By midpoint in the year, staff tensions continued to grow. Among the problem areas staff members wrestled with
were scarcity of supplies and equipment, lack of communication, last-
minute planning, lack of compromise and consensus within teams,
diverse and conflicting understandings of Mega Center's future direction, and lack of closure on issues. While wanting to participate in
decision making, many staff members visualized leadership as a top-
down arrangement and expected Suzanne to address the problems.
After an all-day staff development session on conflict resolution that
exposed these and other areas of concern, Suzanne admitted going
home and internalizing everything the staff had pointed out as issues in
the school. "Everything that was wrong, I owned," she said. "But after
a while," she continued, "I began to see what was mine and what wasn't
mine. That was when I realized my role as leader and decided what I
had to do. . . . That was when I decided to give my I-am-your-leader talk."

At a meeting in early March, Suzanne told the faculty she needed
to clarify a few points on leadership. "I am your leader," she said
emphatically. "And I intend to remain your leader." She introduced a
reading from M. Scott Peck's *The Different Drum* (1987). "This particular section of the book talks about dependency and about building community. And I think that strikes me because we at Mega Center are building a community. Even more important we are building a
family which is even closer knit, a more nurturing society than community." Suzanne began reading:

> A community cannot exist if the members depend upon a leader to lec-
> ture them or to carry their load. . . . Each one of us has no more and no
> less responsibility for the success of our work together. . . . But groups
> do not at first take kindly to being even relatively leaderless. Although it
> does nothing to develop their maturity—indeed it interferes with their
> development—people would generally much rather depend upon a
> leader to tell them what to do than to determine that for themselves.
> . . . Groups rapidly slip into the task-avoidance assumption of depen-
> dency. And until the group grows out of it—until it becomes a commu-
> nity, a group of all leaders—its members will almost invariably misun-
> derstand and resent their nonauthoritarian leader. . . . To lead people
> into community a true leader must discourage dependency and there
> may be no way to do this except to refuse to lead. Paradoxically, the
> strong leader in these instances is she or he who is willing to risk—even
> welcome—the accusation of failing to lead. (pp. 115–116)

Teachers sat quietly at desks arranged in five long straight rows.
Usually faculty meetings were held in rooms where teachers pulled

folding chairs into a large circle, or where they sat at desks arranged in groups of four. Suzanne chose a different room for this meeting. Teachers listened nervously, as Suzanne continued.

> This is the kind of leadership I was expected to provide for this group. . . . I will keep the vision. It is my sacred duty. . . . That is exactly what I should be doing. I shouldn't be worried about the little pieces. I should be worried about the vision because if I don't keep it, it won't be there at all. . . . This is my style of leadership. It is leaderless.

Entangled in conflicting metaphors, Suzanne reached for ways to clarify her role.

Teachers' Reactions. Teachers expressed confusion about Suzanne's message to them. On the one hand, she said they were all leaders and needed to take that responsibility. On the other hand, she held the vision close to herself and saw keeping the vision as her major responsibility. Attempting to find her way through the maze of the year as an empowering leader, she stood in front and told them she would lead them through the maze by keeping the vision before them.

Commenting on Suzanne's description of leaderless leadership, one teacher said,

> I struggle with the concept. There were times when it seemed like it would have been nice to have somebody just say, "This is the way it's going," and to create some order. But I also recognize and appreciate that out of this we will all grow in our ability to be leaders and take leadership roles. . . . We're so used to a situation where we're told what to do and when to do it or how it's going to be done. . . . It's not always going to be comfortable or easy, but that's the way it's going to be.

Hearing Suzanne's explanation of a leaderless leadership, a few teachers understood her to say she considered herself a leaderless leader. They did not grasp her vision of leaderless leadership as a concept empowering all to exercise leadership. Rather, some saw Suzanne's speech as providing a rationale for dysfunction. One teacher expressed her frustration and confusion saying,

> That one bothers me. When somebody tells me she's a leaderless leader, I wonder where we're headed. . . . I've tossed the

idea around in my head quite a bit, and it frightens me a little bit. It makes me uneasy, to tell you the truth. I don't like the concept at all. There's got to be something that sounds a little better than that. I don't know that I like to follow somebody that's leaderless.

One staff member analyzed leaderless leadership from her perspective as leader of a special program. She too used leaderless leadership as style and leaderless leader as role interchangeably.

The leaderless leadership that I envision is one where the leader is able to work with the ideas, the abilities, the skills, the strengths, and the needy areas in each individual to pull out that which is best in everyone. I see the leaderless leader as a facilitator. . . . I think a leaderless leader can build teacher autonomy. And what I mean by autonomy is not that a teacher needs no one else, but rather that teachers are able to be self-analyzing, able to realize what it is that they need and able to ask for what they need. . . . When I reflect on leaders that I think have been very effective, they have been able to individualize with people they are working with. . . . It's not necessarily that those leaders had a style, it's like they have a personhood—a strong sense of who they are as persons that allows them to individualize with people. . . . If they need to have a didactic conversation they will do that. If the conversation is more give and take and co-learning, they can do that.

Conflicting Metaphors. Although teachers discussed Suzanne's leaderless-leadership presentation in twos and threes, they never had the opportunity to react together as a faculty, to question, or to clarify the concept. Suzanne handed them her vision of leadership, and they could accept it or request a transfer out of the school for the coming year. Instead of seeing leadership as an issue for staff discussion, Suzanne chose to define her role and her style for them. How different this approach was from the method she used in August to arrive at the definition of the role of the resource team. When the teachers disagreed with the resource team's understanding of their role, Suzanne urged the staff to discuss the issue, to draw up alternative plans, and, finally, to vote. When questions arose regarding her role and style, she made her speech without allowing dialogue for teachers to come to terms with her vision.

By March Suzanne had defined herself using the metaphor of

vision-keeper and the concept of leaderless leadership, seemingly contradictory roles. The first assumed that she would make key decisions based on the vision and the second pointed toward shared responsibility. She had both hierarchical and participative metaphors in mind and acted out of both sets of beliefs. Her own ambiguity caused stress for herself and brought misunderstanding from others.

LEADING DAY BY DAY

Knowing from her observation of principals over the years and from her academic studies that managerial responsibilities have dominated the daily work of principals (Cuban, 1988b), Suzanne mentally pushed aside that role. Both her outgoing personality and her recent teaching experience made her more comfortable with the roles of effective principals: resource provider, instructional resource, communicator, and visible presence (Smith & Andrews, 1989). She saw herself solving daily problems in the light of the vision, yet the pressures of each day determined Suzanne's schedule and demanded her attention.

Although Suzanne drew her views of principalship from the vision-keeper metaphor and leaderless-leadership concept, the pace and format of her typical day bore striking resemblance to the day of the traditional principal in Harry Wolcott's *The Man in the Principal's Office* (1973). Wolcott reports that the principal in his study spent the vast majority of his time with individuals in brief exchanges, in meetings, and on the telephone. On each of five randomly selected days from February through April, Suzanne handled an average of 10 telephone calls, attended or facilitated 4 or 5 meetings, and held brief discussions with approximately 40 individuals.

Suzanne described her daily activities as chaotic and sometimes overwhelming. She recounted an incident reflecting her experience. One day early in the year, as Suzanne left the school she dropped her calendar-planner in the parking lot. The binder popped open, and the wind scattered the pages on the ground. Looking down on the mess she thought, "This is how life is." Another time she said, "The role of the principal is to think simultaneously on four subjects."

Teachers and parents commented on Suzanne's hectic pace. One teacher said,

When I think of leadership, I think of Suzanne, and I see her running, just running into her office, and here and there. . . .

Maybe too many things were started at a new school the first
year. . . . Maybe the school was pushed here too quickly. . . .
But I think she needs more support.

Another teacher thought district office personnel had Suzanne running around too much. "She needs to be an advocate for Mega Center, but not run around everywhere. She's 500 percent Mega Center,
and that's too much." A parent offered her observation that Suzanne
was very busy, always on the fly, and very rushed. "But she is so enthusiastic and has wonderful ideas," she added. "It seems like she is
Mega Center's philosophy in action," another parent suggested, while
still another remarked that Suzanne and the teachers all seemed overwhelmed.

Teachers wanted Suzanne to provide reassurance and stability.
Parents wanted her to initiate challenging programs for their children.
Teachers needed time away from the public eye to develop programs
and work with the children. Even during the first week of school, visitors asked for an inside look at the school and its programs. Outsiders
remarked on how well the school was running. Insiders felt fragmented and exposed. Teachers rejoiced in their students' achieve-
ments. Parents complained because the school was not everything
they expected. Suzanne encouraged teachers, praising them "for the
magic they were doing with the children." She urged parents to keep
bringing their concerns to the school. "She wants to be supportive to
everybody," remarked one teacher, "but that's impossible." Pulled in
different directions, pushed to respond to diverse expectations, and
buffeted by staff conflict, Suzanne voiced the feeling that she lived from
crisis to crisis.

VISION-KEEPER AND CULTURE

When Suzanne Dawson accepted the position of principal of Mega
Center for Learning, she adopted the vision of its planners as her own.
The metaphors embedded in the school's planning documents—for
example, parents as partners, performance teams of teachers, families of learners, as well as multiple intelligences and children as peak
performers—resonated with her own beliefs and values, and she found
a match she could support and promote.

Teachers came to Mega Center with assorted, diverse, and conflicting ideas on what their new school should be, what they should

do to achieve their goals, and what they needed from each other and from their leader. Their August training plunged them immediately into planning for the students. They were impatient with training that focused on building their cooperative skills.

Suzanne Dawson did not know most of her new teachers personally, but she surmised that they shared the vision of Mega Center she had in her head. At training sessions, district personnel told teachers they were marvelous risk-takers, outstanding educators, and people with a mission. Their mission was making Mega Center come alive and become a model of educational transformation.

Because Suzanne did not know where teachers' images for Mega Center and its operation converged on or diverged from her own, she was surprised when conflicts over the interpretation of the vision erupted. Defending the vision, Suzanne proclaimed herself vision-keeper.

Team membership usually prevented teachers from going to their rooms, shutting the door, and ignoring the prescribed vision. When conflict escalated, Suzanne became more insistent on her role as vision-keeper. She had promised herself and the district that she would implement the vision as she saw it. She did not give sustained attention to any one issue but moved quickly from situation to situation. She seemed unaware that her day-to-day behavior reflected her tight control of the vision and shaped a noncollaborative culture.

In adopting the vision-keeper stance, Suzanne set herself at odds with the vision and with her own beliefs and values. She believed in participative leadership and teacher empowerment. She believed the contours of the vision would change as new research findings surfaced. The vision-keeper metaphor left no room for translating these beliefs into practice.

The culture teachers hoped for was not the culture that developed under Suzanne's leadership. Her vision of schooling may have promoted a collaborative culture. Her vision of leadership gave rise to a culture that stymied effective communication, sharing of power, and interactive decision making.

The question of Mega Center's leadership does not rest solely with consideration of metaphors. The human factors of individual leadership preferences and demands from both inside and outside the institution add complexity to the consideration of leadership. However, Mega Center's vision would be enhanced if the leader found new metaphors for her leadership role.

Several contemporary writers place the leader at the heart of the school, listening to the beat (Blackmore, 1989; Hartsock, 1983; Sergiovanni, 1992a). Here leadership is an organic, intrinsic, and moral function, rather than an extrinsic one of leading the troops through the maze. Here the vision becomes a palpable spirit, bonding children, teachers, principal, parents, and the community. All become vision-keepers.

CHAPTER NINE

Reform and Metaphor

The voices of Mega Center planners, principal, parents, and teachers speak at a particular time in the history of education in the United States, a time during which the words *educational reform* appear almost daily in the newspaper. The history of reform does not reflect a linear process in which one improvement effort followed another. Rather, reform efforts have represented eclectic attempts to improve one or another aspect of schooling. Researchers have suggested multiple visions of reform based on the perspectives of their studies.

This chapter draws connections between metaphors that emerged during Mega Center's startup year and images of schooling revealed in the history of reform. It also discusses Mega Center's beginnings in relationship to metaphors in selected educational literature on improving schools. Finally, since this case study provides an example of relationships between the language of reform and reform efforts, the chapter concludes with reflections on building a culture to strengthen these relationships.

MEGA CENTER AND THE HISTORY OF REFORM

"We, the children, parents, educators and community members, working together as a FAMILY OF LEARNERS nurture an enthusiasm for lifelong learning. Using our knowledge and understanding, we commit ourselves to excellence!" This statement of Mega Center's mission, with the words *family of learners* printed in bold capital letters on its promotional brochure, exposed an image of schooling that challenges the longstanding institutional mold. School district planners envisioned the school as breaking through conceptual barriers to effect change and as constructing a new model for education. The principal and teachers hoped Mega Center would become a well-known model of educational excellence.

The family-of-learners metaphor stands in sharp contrast with the notions of schooling that have prevailed in the United States since the mid-1800s, as presented in Chapter 3. Beginning with the construction of Quincy School in Boston, in 1848, most schools throughout the country have looked virtually the same, with separate classrooms, uniform curricula, textbooks, tests, and promotions from grade to grade. Common schools proposed to produce moral citizens with reading and math skills enabling them to enter the work force and to participate in political life (Tyack et al., 1980). Teachers performed tasks of intellectual overseers, drillmasters, and interpreters of culture (Cuban, 1993).

The writings of Elwood Cubberley and John Dewey represent the two strands of the Progressive Era. Drawing on the school-as-factory metaphor, Cubberley likened children to raw materials that education shapes and fashions into finished products (Cremin, 1988). Scientific management principles and hierarchical bureaucratic models influenced his thought. Dewey espoused an organic growth metaphor, viewing school as a social institution that immerses children in an embryonic social life. In his view, schools exist to nurture the intellectual, moral, and aesthetic development of children.

A plethora of educational reforms with no single focus has swept the United States since the 1950s. Employing the factory metaphor, *A Nation at Risk* (NCEE, 1983) gave voice to the nation's growing dissatisfaction with education. The report viewed teachers as laborers whose productivity should be measured by examining the quality of the students through testing. Many of the country's most recent reform initiatives are compatible with the national educational goals delineated in *America 2000: An Education Strategy* (U.S. Department of Education, 1991). The document called for communities throughout the United States to break the mold and to create a new generation of American schools.

Examining Mega Center's initial plan, an outside observer might cite the school as an example of significant change in education. Its arrangement of teachers in teams and students in multi-age groups, its inclusion of parents and the community, its thematic, interdisciplinary curriculum, and its experience-based learning model provide evidence of deviations from the practices of the common school and from the norm of what still happens in most schools. However, a look from a closer perspective reveals that significant change involves more than designing and implementing new practices. Some of the tensions, struggles, and failures of reform efforts come from discrepancies between the metaphors of planners and implementors as well as divergence among personal metaphors of those involved in the implementation process.

Moving Beyond the Common School to Dewey

Calling themselves a family of learners did not ensure that Mega Center implementors realized the full implications of the metaphor. They had not explored what the metaphor revealed about schooling and what aspects of school the metaphor hid.

Teachers, parents, and principal negotiated their way through each day using their personal metaphors to give meaning and coherence to their lives at school. At times their dialogue and practice disclosed metaphors consistent with conventional ideas about school, notions congruent with the common school, instilled in them through cultural experience and reinforced by professional practice and political rhetoric. Yet both teachers and parents envisioned enhanced roles for themselves and challenging opportunities for the children. They trusted that Mega Center would move beyond the common school concept.

The progressive educational philosophy of John Dewey influenced Mega Center planners. Explaining the school's theoretical underpinnings, Paul Elson, one of Mega Center's architects, commented, "Dewey's research and Dewey's work on experience and experiential learning is powerful . . . it's as good as anything out there now." Mega Center adopted Dewey's experiential methodology as its primary mode of instruction. At another level, both Dewey's view of enculturation and Paul Elson's notion of ever-widening circles, from family to community, to society, to world, exemplified an organic growth metaphor.

Resisting Managerial Functions

Mega Center's principal disavowed the strand of progressivism based on scientific management and hierarchical bureaucracy as a function of her leadership. However, the notion of principal as vision-keeper preserved vestiges of hierarchical thinking. Teachers displayed ambivalence, both resisting decisions made without their consultation and calling for the principal to assert her authority. Neither the principal nor the teachers envisioned cohesive leadership metaphors. Since the teachers and principal did not discuss their leadership metaphors, they lost an opportunity to uncover one source of dissonance.

Paul Elson affirmed that the district did not want a seasoned ad-

ministrator who had preconceived ideas. He believed Suzanne
Dawson's style fit Mega Center and Mega Center's style fit Suzanne.
"She does an incredibly fine job of keeping the torch lit," he commented, "and holding it in front of the people, which is a hard job for
an administrator and one that a lot of them tend not to do well." He
continued, emphasizing the importance of moving administration
away from strictly managerial functions: "School administrators tend
to get submerged in managerial aspects of the job, which is easy, and
it's very difficult to stand out there with that torch every single day
and keep waving it, and also keep it full of fuel."

As shaper of Mega Center's vision, Paul Elson surely realized the
centrality of the family-of-learners metaphor. Yet he used torch-bearer
as a primary metaphor for the school's leadership. The incongruity
between the notions of heading a family and being in the forefront of
a campaign, crusade, or movement not only suggests a political
agenda, but also indicates the need for reflection on the connotations
of metaphorical language.

While Paul's torch-bearer metaphor moves the principalship away
from managerial responsibilities, it is not a metaphor he discussed with
Suzanne and the Mega Center staff. His style-match comment revealed
the underlying belief that, given sufficient time and effort, putting the
right pieces together would result in the desired outcome. Paul's
metaphors for leadership, Suzanne's images of her role, and the teachers' expectations of the principal not only differed, but sometimes
contradicted one another. To release themselves from the management or leadership debate, Mega Center teachers, principal, and key
district office personnel needed to engage in a dialogue on leadership
that would move them beyond top-down models of the school-as-
factory metaphor. Without discussion, they would not see the internal inconsistencies of the metaphors behind their language.

Striving for Excellence

Throughout his professional life, Paul Elson dedicated his energies to breaking the mold and creating a new generation of American
schools. This was his focus long before it became the nation's agenda.
Suzanne and the Mega Center teachers also saw themselves in the
vanguard of American education. Before the announcement of national
goals, Mega Center proposed to lead the way in educational excellence.

But even the notion of excellence connoted a wide variety of
beliefs and values, especially between teachers and parents. Teach-

ers explained excellence as understanding new concepts, integrating content and skills, producing a creative project, delving deeply into a topic, mastering new skills, thinking critically and flexibly, being an independent and motivated learner, and doing one's best work. Some parents worried that in pursuing creative endeavors, children would miss learning critical skills necessary for future success. Behind the teachers' and parents' descriptions lay student-as-lifelong-learner and student-as-future-worker images. Because these are not necessarily contradictory images, they could have been placed side-by-side, informing a discussion of educational priorities.

Vigorous debate about the meaning of excellence occurred at Mega Center's Parent Advisory Committee meetings. Although Suzanne Dawson listened to the parents' discussion and explained Mega Center's vision, no consensus on the meaning of excellence came from the conversation. In arguing about definitions, neither principal nor parents recognized the need to examine underlying metaphors and assumptions. They missed a chance to understand how their metaphors influenced their perception of Mega Center's vision.

Although Mega Center's emphasis on excellence differed from the national discourse, it encompassed compatible ideas. *America 2000* calls for children to "demonstrate competency in challenging subject matter including English, mathematics, science, history, and geography" (U.S. Department of Education, 1991, p. 3). Mega Center's plan included challenging each child to achieve excellence while making choices and pursuing personal interests within an integrated curriculum. Implementation of the school's plan may be one way of reaching the *America 2000* goals.

Understanding Diverse Metaphors

As Mega Center forged its way through its first year, time after time teachers, parents, and principal faced the challenge of understanding one another's language. Based on differing beliefs and values, the same words created a maze of diverse meanings and conflicting metaphors. For example, the Explore Room controversy discussed in Chapter 6 involved seeing time spent in the room through different lenses. Some saw it as extended playtime; others perceived it as wasted school time; still others understood it as an enrichment time for children to explore areas of interest. Metaphors such as school-as-workplace-for-children or school-as-land-of-opportunity undergirded perceptual differences and accounted for strong positive or negative reactions from teachers and parents.

The history of American education provided no clear path through the linguistic maze since it represents neither evolution of thought nor nationally agreed upon ideas regarding the purposes of education. Without time and opportunity to clarify their metaphors and share their visions, Mega Center teachers, parents, and principal would continue to meet obstacles on their way through the maze.

MEGA CENTER AND SCHOOL TRANSFORMATION

Paul Elson saw Mega Center as "an experiment at transformation . . . maybe setting a new standard of what can happen in a school and what can happen to learning when you pay attention to what works and when you pay attention to how human beings learn." Paul characterized Mega Center as "one of the lead wagons on a journey of school transformation." Following Paul's idea, Mega Center's teachers and principal proudly described the school's programs and their practices as based on current research on how children learn. For example, they told visitors that the research findings of Howard Gardner (1985) on multiple intelligences formed a basis for their decisions regarding curriculum and program development.

Addressing Multiple Intelligences

Although bulletin boards in many classrooms contained displays enumerating Gardner's seven kinds of intelligence, teachers expressed a wide range of familiarity with Gardner's work. Some reported that their summer training included ideas from Gardner. In addition to the training experience, other teachers had read one or more of his books. Some used the term *intelligences* synonymously with *learning styles,* while others spoke of physically active children as "bodily-kinesthetic."

While the rhetoric of spokespersons for Mega Center reinforced the multiple-intelligences metaphor, the influence of Howard Gardner's research findings on teachers' practice varied from classroom to classroom. The leverage of the language of multiple intelligences convinced several parents to enroll their children at Mega Center, but conflicting visions reflected divergent metaphors.

Notions regarding the purposes of schooling formed the backdrop for differing views on how Mega Center implemented its promise to address children's multiple intelligences. Thinking of the school as land of opportunity, some parents thought the school would identify and foster their children's special intelligences. For example, they expected that children who showed a preference for music would have multiple opportunities to participate in musical activities. Gardner (1985) describes the bodily-kinesthetic intelligence as the ability to use the body in highly differentiated and skilled ways for goal-directed purposes. Parents whose children displayed skills in this intelligence expected that Mega Center would provide programs for dance, drama, and athletics. Discord and disappointment arose when practice and programs did not meet expectations.

Mega Center did meet the expectations of parents who had another view of how the school would address their children's learning needs. These parents conceived of the school as providing all children with chances to explore music, art, drama, movement, athletics, language, and mathematics within the integrated, thematic curriculum. They expected teachers to infuse learning activities with experiences beyond textbooks and worksheets. These parents expressed greater satisfaction since their notions of what would happen at Mega Center were closer to the teachers' ideas and practices. Many of these parents looked to the school as a broker that would direct them toward community resources to augment their children's interests and talents. Mega Center could have capitalized on the congruence of these teachers' and parents' metaphors, shedding light on discussions of the purposes of schooling.

Leading Toward a Shared Vision

Suzanne Dawson described Mega Center as a school on the cutting edge of educational innovation. She realized that change was a process, not an event. She gave staff members license and leeway to transform education for the children. Without the practical experience of knowing how the implications of transforming education for children can challenge traditional school structures and professional relationships, at times she found herself in the midst of a maze. Though she attempted to use the light of the vision to find the way through the maze, not everyone would follow because her vision was not their vision.

For Mega Center to succeed, Suzanne Dawson needed to follow the advice offered by Senge (1990). "Building shared vision must be seen as a central element of the daily work of leaders," he argues. "It is ongoing and never-ending. . . . Ultimately, leaders intent on building shared visions must be willing to continually share their personal visions. They must be prepared to ask, 'Will you follow me?'" (pp. 214–215). Developing a shared vision is a complex process requiring time for individuals to explore their varying metaphors for schooling. The process demands the ability to argue respectfully, to concede graciously, and to prevail unceremoniously. Arriving at a shared vision necessitates both trust and mature, professional behavior on the part of all participants.

Since Mega Center was "an early baby," the staff needed additional maturation time to develop its family relationships, norms, and practices. They needed an interplay of dialogue and practice away from the public eye to generate an ideological stance that could be sustained by their professional relationships and could be made visible in their norms and practices.

With close and explicit relationships and partnerships with parents and the community as the school's immediate goal, Mega Center became too public too soon. While teachers experienced boundary crossing and intrusion by parents, parents sought greater participation in schoolwide decision making as well as in the process of their own children's education. The principal invited the involvement of parents in areas traditionally reserved for teachers—sometimes before, often without, discussion with the teachers.

Changing the Role of Teacher

New models for schools require changes in the role of the teacher (Johnson, 1990). Mega Center teachers expected that their new school would demand adjustments in their understanding and practice of the role of teacher, but they did not anticipate the sources of the pressure for change. With conflicting metaphors on the roles of parents and teachers, Mega Center developed practices that supported neither the professional role of teachers nor the participative role of parents.

An example of the confusion caused by conflicting metaphors and unreflective practice occurred when children moved from one family of learners to another. Perceiving themselves as partners and decision makers in their children's education, parents came to school and told the principal they wanted their children moved to another family. The principal made arrangements for the move, often without discussion with either or both of the home-base teachers. Seeing themselves as professionals who should have been consulted before the move, the teachers felt their professional expertise was undermined. Unexamined metaphors produced practices at odds with the cooperative spirit of Mega Center's overarching family metaphor.

The road to uniting the family and the school "is far more difficult and tortuous than is even hinted at in the second-wave rhetoric, in part because teachers are not being prepared to walk it" (Goodlad, 1990, p. 253). Although Goodlad's comment refers primarily to the initial preparation of teachers, experienced teachers need to make deep changes in their understandings of their roles. The path through that maze of change is tortuous for teachers.

Sara Lawrence Lightfoot (1983) uses the metaphor of mixing parts to produce a whole to describe a good school. She includes people and structures as two significant pieces of the whole. Seeing their role as responsible professionals, Mega Center's teachers centered their energies on teaching the children, but many expressed confusion about the roles of other persons on the staff, such as an office worker who functioned as assistant principal and the members of the resource team who requested reassignment early in the year. At a faculty meeting the principal offered to clarify the confusion for anyone who wanted to ask her, since she had responsibility for job assignments. Meanwhile, she tended to another piece of the whole, focusing primarily on preserving and promoting the school's ideology. While school personnel needed the latitude to use experience as a guide in arranging the parts to form a cohesive whole, initial clarifications of roles and structures would not have prevented future reconsiderations and would have averted continuing misunderstandings.

The findings of Michael Rutter and his associates (1979) corroborate Lightfoot's (1983) conclusion that teachers see consideration for their professional needs as nurturance. Although Mega Center teachers and principal expected each other to be nurturing toward the children, the staff as a whole did not extend professional sustenance to each other. Because teachers divided into teams during the August orientation experience, they initially pursued building relationships within their team. When conflicts arose on teams, some members sought others outside their teams for personal and professional support. While teachers found support where they could, the staff continued to be fragmented. Building cohesion, trust, and collegiality would require that teachers and principal continue to invest time in fashioning and fostering their professional relationships and in providing for teacher's professional needs.

Mega Center's initial blueprints carried mixed metaphors. The school's principal, teachers, and parents held diverse personal metaphors. The school's culture, with its norms and practices, developed from a complex multiplicity of personal beliefs and values as well as from the institutionalization of foundational language. The school's efforts to transform education for children had to be illumined by thoughtful consideration of both personal and institutional metaphorical language. With the power generated by the language of a growing shared vision, Mega Center could find its way through the maze.

METAPHORS AND REFORMING SCHOOL CULTURE

"Words alone don't change reality. But changes in our conceptual system do change what is real for us and affect how we perceive the world and act upon those perceptions" (Lakoff & Johnson, 1980, pp. 145–146). Transporting Lakoff and Johnson's statement into an educational setting sheds light on the phenomenon of reforming school culture. The language of school reform remains political rhetoric unless conceptual transformation occurs for individuals engaged in the school-change process.

If Mega Center is determined to provide alternative ways for children to learn and if it is to become a model of successful school reform, the school will have to thoughtfully examine its language, including words that have become jargon, such as *bodily-kinesthetic*, and words that never took hold, such as *educator*. However, beyond recognizing jargon and dead language lie deeper issues.

Moving Toward Conceptual Transformation

For Mega Center to grow toward becoming a school of excellence, teachers and principal must engage in a process of continuing conceptual transformation. One teacher expressed her view of Mega Center as a lab school, with teachers always ready to listen to findings of studies on educational issues and willing to consider how the study results could affect classroom practice.

Taking this teacher's suggestion, Mega Center teachers and principal could view the school as a laboratory of school transformation. The laboratory concept could give focus to the school's change efforts and could provide the vehicle for examining the school's dominant metaphors and for considering how the metaphors support or stymie practice. Teachers and principal could interact, at various times, with parents, community members, business persons, school district representatives, and nearby college and university personnel, sharing perceptions and perspectives on improving education for Mega Center's students. Through these efforts personal visions could become visible, and shared visions could emerge.

The laboratory could include components missing in Mega Center's first year: integrated and sustained staff development and developmental evaluation. Staff development is not only a way to build knowledge, skills, and attitudes that would strengthen the school's program components, but also "an unfreezing influence that gets people to consider large-scale restructuring" (Owen, Loucks-Horsley, & Horsley, 1991, p. 11). Integrated staff development consists not of piecemeal, isolated experiences, but of in-depth opportunities for growth arising from the needs of the group. Sustained staff development gives participants opportunities to implement ideas in the classroom, to reflect on successes and shortcomings, to receive assistance in refining practices, and to enjoy support from colleagues and principal during the implementation process. With an integrated and sustained staff development process at the heart of a school's restructuring effort, stakeholders can become a community of lifelong learners.

Mega Center's planners and district personnel expected the principal and teachers to break the mold of traditional schooling. Paul Elson stood ready to articulate the school's beliefs, to support the principal's and teachers' efforts, and to bring in resource persons to provide assistance and direction. Even with these resources, a second component missing at Mega Center was developmental evaluation. Unlike an evaluation that provides information based on collected data at the end of the process, developmental evaluation intimately involves stakeholders in a collaborative inquiry process (Stockdill, Duhon-Sells, Olson, & Patton, 1992). The evaluator collects and communicates data on a regular basis and facilitates processes enabling persons to articulate and to resolve differing or conflicting views (Preskill, in press). An ongoing developmental evaluation process would support the principal's and teachers' attempts at addressing critical issues.

Addressing Mega Center's Issues

Commitment to a process of examining how personal and institutional metaphors reflect beliefs and values and shape practice would close the gap between planning and implementation. When school districts initiate reform efforts, planners give voice to their visions of transformation of education. Embedded in the articulation of visions for reform are institutional metaphors, shared only by those collaborating in their development. Neither planners nor implementors can assume there is metaphorical alignment with the vision among the participants in the reform effort. Nor can those assigned to lead the implementation disregard the continuing need to articulate prevailing metaphors with teachers and parents, exposing what elements of reform the metaphors reveal and what aspects of the project they hide.

Adjusting Institutional Language. Since a single metaphor reveals some, but not all, aspects of a reality, institutionally crafted language may fall short of describing experience. Implementors may adjust institutional language to reflect their experience or they may propose new language to express reformulated concepts. When implementors discover a gap between their experience and prevailing metaphors, new language naming the experience may not be readily available. The new language may emerge as conceptualization clarifies.

Mega Center's principal and teachers face the challenge of finding language to express their concept of leadership. Exploration of the issue would ease the tension and confusion brought on by conflicting ideas about leadership. It would enable the principal to hear what teachers need from their leader as they engage in the complex professional challenge of forming a new school. The discussion may lead the teachers to realize what leadership they could ask of each other as they recognize their own power as leaders.

A second hurdle confronting Mega Center is elucidating the family-of-learners and team metaphors. Teachers and principal must decide whether *family* really can include children, educators, parents, and community members, and whether *team* can encompass teachers, interns, aides, a learning specialist, and volunteers, when the experience of the first year did not reflect this inclusion. At stake is the adequacy of the current institutional language describing the reality. With new language the staff could address issues such as boundary crossing with more clarity and objectivity.

Mega Center's implementors called their working groups *teams*, not *performance teams*, as the startup documents did. Seeing no need for the additional word, and having previous experiences as members of teams, the teachers did not use the word *performance* to describe their teams. The nuances of the word eluded them as they strained to set the school year in motion. Because individuals had varying notions of team, and because team members held differing ideas about the school's vision and its implementation, even the metaphor of team did not provide sufficient anchor to sustain all teams in their working together. As Mega Center teachers examine their functioning as teams, they might consider whether the concept of performance teams would enhance their practice.

When metaphorical language reflects conceptual congruence,

new practice can develop. The language not only signifies the new practice, but also strengthens it, as the language relates the practice to the institutional vision. All implementors become spokespersons for the vision, and find meaning for their professional practice in its expression.

Capitalizing on the Family Metaphor for Children. Mega Center's principal and teachers demonstrated extraordinary success in developing an environment and practices consistent with their metaphor of children as families of learners. Their practice reflected their language in the stimulating, homey environment they created for the children, in the engaging conversation they held with the children, and in the useful skills they taught the children. Capitalizing on the harmony between beliefs and practice reflected in this metaphor, principal and teachers have a model for examining their other institutional metaphors.

Reform language is short-lived when it does not reflect the thinking of implementors. Some reform efforts fail because implementors see no reason to change. Current practices work for them. They have not adopted new metaphors and see the language of reform as jargon imposed from above.

At times, implementors take on a new practice willingly, although they may be skeptical of the outcome. A carefully tended implementation process can sustain change in practice and lead practitioners to new conceptualizations of their role. Without support during the implementation phase and without adequate time to integrate changes into their personal belief systems, teachers return to former practices, the reform effort fades, and the language dies.

Cross-age grouping provides an example of a practice that was new for most Mega Center teachers. Some said they were uncertain about how they could teach a wide age span of children. Arrangements of children in cross-age groups provoked controversy in some teams. But Suzanne encouraged and facilitated thoughtful discussion among the teachers on this issue, and she urged them to be vigilant about the effects of this arrangement on the children's learning. Even early in the year, teachers began to realize the benefits of multi-age groupings for children. Children grew in their sense of responsibility for one another, they looked to each other for coaching and mentoring, and they moved readily from group to group within their family as their instructional needs warranted. Under the umbrella of the family-of-learners metaphor, the multi-age grouping concept found a home and provided a framework for successful practice.

The language of reform is a gateway to examining institutional beliefs and practices. Knowledge of the language enables an individual to participate in conversation about the institution and gives the person power to critique its practices. But knowing the language differs from sharing the beliefs.

Like all reform efforts, Mega Center will have its critics. Those who are not patient with first-year shortcomings and those who do not hold Mega Center's assumptions may have much to criticize. But those who are dedicated to Mega Center's beliefs and values will commit themselves to a process of growth that includes reflective examination of personal and institutional metaphors.

Epilogue

Prior to the last faculty meeting of the year, I asked Suzanne if I could bring a thank-you treat for the faculty and staff and say a few words of appreciation to them. When it came to my turn on the agenda, I thanked them for their gracious hospitality, for their openness with me, and for the precious gift of their time. "It is with deep gratitude," I said, "that I take what you have given me and go to write the story of Mega Center's first year." I had brought five books as gifts for them to use with the children. Accompanying each book was a small card with a message reflecting my admiration for them. I promised I would see them again.

Despite the difficulties of the first year, both Suzanne and the teachers had a sincere desire to succeed in this venture. They had cooperated fully in allowing me to observe in their classrooms, attend their meetings, and conduct interviews with them, trusting that the results of the study would provide a resource they could consider in making plans for future improvement. Before moving to the next agenda item, Suzanne Dawson thanked me for choosing Mega Center as a study site, saying,

> Think of the growth we'll have, being able to stand back and see ourselves. How many people get a mirror to look in! And that's really what it is. And I know because of the integrity that you show, the piece that you produce will be one that will be honest, but it won't be something that points fingers. We'll be able to see where the warts are and where the beauty is and say "Yah!" Recognizing ourselves in your work, we will be able to say, "Now that we know this, what can we do?"

Throughout the year teachers had commented on the value of having someone from the outside in their school regularly. They had expressed appreciation when I listened both in informal situations and in scheduled interviews. Remarks such as "You are a nice sounding board," "This has been good; it's like therapy," "Thank you for being here and for listening," and "We're lucky to have you. This is good for Mega Center. . . . I've been hearing wonderful things about this interview, so I can't wait" had preceded or concluded many interviews.

Several teachers had spoken of trusting me as a researcher who would respect their confidentiality and protect their anonymity when they described sensitive aspects of Mega Center's first year from their perspective during formal interviews: "I know I can trust you, I have the sense I can"; "I haven't shown this to anyone else . . . "; "Knowing who you are I trust you."

From the beginning many teachers had asked if they would have access to the results of my study. One teacher, Mary Lee Kline, commented,

> You've got this catbird's seat, this bird's eye view of what's going on, and I can't wait to read what you write. People have talked about their meeting with Jean. I think everybody's being honest with you. You're probably getting more than anybody in this building is getting as far as everybody's real honest, gut feeling about it.

Commenting further on my perspective, another person had said,

> I'm really anxious to read your paper, to get your input. Frankly, I'm just dying to know how you see it because you're not really an outsider to us. You've been part of the family since the beginning but you're also an unbiased outsider. I think that perspective will be invaluable.

As I thought back on my year at Mega Center I asked myself several questions. Why would these people open their professional lives to me as they launched a new venture? Most were experienced professionals and knew their days would be busy and stressful enough without someone watching. Why would they let me see what they called their "warts and pimples"? They were people accustomed to success in their professional lives and they gave unbounded energy to make Mega Center successful. Why would they eagerly await my analysis when they knew that honest reporting would include stories of conflict?

Perhaps the answer rests partially in their intuition that something magical actually was happening–it certainly was happening for many,

many children. But beyond that, perhaps they had a glimmer of the possibility of fulfilling their mission to become a worldwide model of educational excellence. They were putting in place the core of a superior way of educating children—a nurturing environment, an integrated curriculum, experiential learning opportunities, choices for children. They were in the process of shedding the shackles of old language, old practices, old beliefs. Part of the pain was in not having tried-and-true language and practices to put in their place, so they questioned their changing beliefs. But the bridge between belief and practice is metaphor, and as they would become more comfortable with their new metaphors, their professional lives could take on fresh meaning and deep satisfaction. They were courageous people, willing to let down their guard in front of a seasoned educator-become-researcher.

In the end, it may or may not be that other schools will look like Mega Center. But one of Mega Center's contributions to educational reform could be to enable other schools to see the value of examining their practices and beliefs through the prism of their metaphors. When schools do this, they become both more reflective and more intentional in how they set about educating the families of children in their care.

Although this study concentrated on Mega Center's first year, readers may wonder how Mega Center fared in subsequent years. In a telephone conversation, Suzanne Dawson highlighted developments in Mega Center's second and third years.

In year two, 1991–1992, the school housed kindergarten through fourth grade as planned. Two families of learners became K–4 families, and two families remained K–3. Because of this expansion as well as a large kindergarten enrollment, the average class size grew from 20 to 26. Three teachers requested transfer from the building, the two who left the resource team early in the year and one home-base teacher. After Suzanne and a committee of teachers interviewed 80 applicants, she hired five new teachers.

Two programatic changes occurred in the second year. Based on faculty recommendation, Suzanne eliminated the resource-team concept and created more traditional roles for three specialists with music, bodily-kinesthetic, and art backgrounds. The second change occurred in the use of the Explore Room. A teacher aide staffed the room, and teachers had assigned times when they could bring their students. As the year went on, teachers used the room less frequently.

Year two was a transition year from an active parent advisory committee whose primary responsibility was to coordinate its activities with the principal and teachers to a site-based council whose mandate included interaction with the district on a policy level. Since the site-based council needed time to organize and to discuss its charter, the parent advisory committee remained the stronger and more active body during this year. One action of the parent advisory committee involved hiring consultants to address the ongoing issue of staff conflict. Near the end of the school year, two consultants interviewed all staff members, then wrote a report, which they presented to a joint parent and faculty committee during the summer of 1992. The consultants presented a summary of their report to the entire faculty during the August orientation prior to year three.

Despite the inner turmoil, two events promoted a sense of community among Mega Center stakeholders. The first was the building of a large playground on the school property. Parents, teachers, students, and community members worked with an architect to design the playground, and volunteers did the construction work. A second major event was an all-school carnival to raise money to support the American Women's Trans-Antarctic Expedition led by Ann Bancroft, the first woman to reach both the North and South Poles. Working with teachers and with the help of their parents, students designed all games and planned the concessions. "This event created a wonderful spirit of community," Suzanne reflected. The students' involvement extended beyond contributing money to the expedition: During the next school year, from November 1992 until January 14, 1993, they tracked the four women's 660-mile trek by ski to the science station at the South Pole.

In April 1992 I met with Suzanne, gave her a copy of my manuscript, and asked if, after she had read it, she would give me her reactions to what I had written. She called in August, inviting me to present my findings to the faculty in a one-hour session during orientation week. My presentation was back-to-back with the report of the consultants on conflict resolution.

Suzanne described the third year, 1992–1993, as a personnel nightmare. Three teachers resigned during the first month of the school year, two for personal reasons and a third in order to take advantage of a professional opportunity. Another five teachers left the school during ensuing months, two of whom took positions at the district office in curriculum and staff development. The district was slow to authorize Suzanne to hire replacements, and parents complained bitterly. Five of the teachers who left in year three were original Mega Center teachers.

Mega Center's student population continued to grow. The school now included fifth-graders, and Suzanne created an intermediate team of five teachers. In addition, the teachers whose specialty was kindergarten convinced Suzanne to allow them to form a team of four and to work with a family of kindergartners only. Reluctantly Suzanne agreed when the teachers promised they would create connections with first- through third-grade families as the year progressed. Teachers and parents liked the new arrangement, but the promised connections with the other families never developed.

In year three use of the Explore Room was discontinued. Although the space and materials remained available and teachers could sign up to use the room, teachers did not bring their students there.

A highlight of the year for Suzanne was Howard Gardner's October half-day visit to the school. In the area for a conference, he spent time in each classroom asking questions and affirming the work of the teachers. In the afternoon Suzanne participated on a panel with him.

By the end of the third year several program components were firmly in place: arranging children in families of learners and the accompanying family culture for the students; emphasizing the Mega-Skills as essential competencies for primary-age children; focusing on teaching through the seven kinds of intelligence and providing musical, bodily-kinesthetic, and spatial as well as linguistic and logical-mathematical experiences for the students; using conflict-resolution techniques as the underpinning for the school's discipline policies and procedures; developing strong thematic units of instruction; and initiating a process of portfolio and performance assessment. Proud of Mega Center's growth and seeing the 100 percent commitment of a significant core of parents, Suzanne decided the time was right to take a sabbatical. "I'm a much better designer and planter," she explained to her successor. "You planted the seeds in the garden and it's growing," the new principal replied. "We'll continue to water and weed."

A parent called Suzanne after the first meeting of the site-based council in the 1993–1994 school year to tell her of what the council called their "fortuitous dilemma." During Suzanne's tenure at Mega Center, she had spoken to parents of her hopes and dreams for the school, giving them many more ideas than could be implemented during the first three years. The parent said the council realized that because of Suzanne's influence, it had "about ten years worth of vision. We realized we need to decide what to do with it! And we know that vision needs to be continually under re-vision."

Year four saw the departure of one more of Mega Center's original teachers. Now half were gone, and ten remained. In 1993–1994 the Mega Center Middle School program was in its first year of operation at a site a few miles away from Mega Center. Both schools included sixth-graders. The Mega Center High School program was on the drawing board for possible opening in 1996–1997.

In December 1993, Mega Center received word that it had won a $200,000 grant from the New American Schools Development Corporation. Making the announcement, school officials said the grant monies would allow Mega Center to be free from traditional bureaucracy and constraints. A newspaper account reported the lofty claim that now the school could come closer to its vision and to its goal of enabling students to meet or exceed world-class standards. With the grant monies, Mega Center could become a year-round learning center for the entire community.

With this new opportunity Mega Center will have to attend to the congruence between the metaphors of the learning-center planners and the metaphors of the implementors and stakeholders. Like Mega Center, all schools seriously seeking to educate children for the twenty-first century will have to journey through the maze of school reform.

References

Angus, L. (1989). 'New' leadership and the possibility of educational reform. In J. Smyth (Ed.), *Critical perspectives on educational leadership* (pp. 63-92). New York: The Falmer Press.

Baker, P. J. (1991). Metaphors of mindful engagement and a vision of better schools. *Educational Leadership, 48*, 32-35.

Beck, L. G., & Murphy, J. (1993). *Understanding the principalship: Metaphorical themes, 1920s-1990s*. New York: Teachers College Press.

Bennis, W., & Nanus, B. (1985). *Leaders: The strategies for taking charge*. New York: Harper and Row.

Bestor, A. (1953). *Educational wastelands: The retreat from learning in our public schools*. Urbana: University of Illinois Press.

Black, M. (1979). More about metaphor. In A. Ortony (Ed.), *Metaphor and thought* (pp. 19-43). Cambridge: Cambridge University Press.

Blackmore, J. (1989). Educational leadership: A feminist critique and reconstruction. In J. Smyth (Ed.), *Critical perspectives on educational leadership* (pp. 93-129). New York: The Falmer Press.

Bogdan, R. C., & Biklen, S. K. (1982). *Qualitative research for education: An introduction to theory and methods*. Boston: Allyn and Bacon.

Burbules, N. C. (1993). *Dialogue in teaching: Theory and practice*. New York: Teachers College Press.

Chubb, J. E., & Moe, T. M. (1990). *Politics, markets, and America's schools*. Washington, DC: The Brookings Institute.

Cinnamond, J. (1987). *Metaphors as understanding: Recent reform reports on education* (Report No. HE 020 343). San Diego, CA: Association for the Study of Higher Education. (ERIC Document Reproduction Service No. ED 281 439)

Comer, J. (1980). *School power*. New York: The Free Press.

Commission on the Reorganization of Secondary Education. (1918). *The cardinal principles of secondary education* (Bureau of Education Bulletin No. 35). Washington, DC: U.S. Government Printing Office.

Conant, J. B. (1959). *The American high school today: A first report to interested citizens*. New York: McGraw-Hill.

Cremin, L. A. (1988). *American education: The metropolitan experience 1876-1980*. New York: Harper and Row.

Cuban, L. (1988a). Constancy and change in schools (1880s to the present). In P. W. Jackson (Ed.), *Contributing to educational change* (pp. 85–105). Berkeley: McCutchan Publishing Company.

Cuban, L. (1988b). *The managerial imperative and the practice of leadership in schools*. Albany: State University of New York Press.

Cuban, L. (1993). *How teachers taught: Constancy and change in American classrooms, 1880–1990* (2nd ed.). New York: Teachers College Press.

Cubberley, E. (1916). *Public school administration*. Boston: Houghton Mifflin.

Dewey, J. (1916). *Democracy and education*. Toronto, Ontario: Collier-Macmillan.

Dewey, J. (1972). My pedagogic creed. In J. A. Boydston (Ed.), *The early works 1882–1898* (Vol. 5, pp. 84–95). Carbondale: Southern Illinois University Press.

Doyle, D. P., & Hartle, T. W. (1985). *Excellence in education: The states take charge*. Washington, DC: American Enterprise Institute for Public Policy Research.

Eisner, E. W. (1991). *The enlightened eye: Qualitative inquiry and the enhancement of educational practice*. New York: Macmillan Publishing Company.

Fetterman, D. M. (1989). *Ethnography step by step*. Newbury Park, CA: Sage Publications.

Fullan, M. G. (1991). *The new meaning of educational change* (2nd ed.). New York: Teachers College Press.

Gardner, H. (1985). *Frames of mind: The theory of multiple intelligences*. New York: Basic Books.

Giroux, H. A. (1981). *Ideology, culture and the process of schooling*. Philadelphia: Temple University Press.

Goodlad, J. I. (1984). *A place called school*. New York: McGraw-Hill.

Goodlad, J. I. (1990). *Teachers for our nation's schools*. San Francisco: Jossey-Bass Publishers.

Hall, G. E., & Hord, S. M. (1987). *Change in schools: Facilitating the process*. Albany: State University of New York Press.

Harragan, B. L. (1982). Women and men at work: Jockeying for position. In J. Farley (Ed.), *The woman in management: Career and family issues* (pp. 12–20). Ithaca: IUR Press.

Hartsock, N. (1983). *Money, sex and power: Towards a feminist historical materialism*. New York: Longman.

Jacob, E. (1987). Qualitative research traditions: A review. *Review of Educational Research, 54*, 1–50.

Johnson, S. M. (1990). *Teachers at work: Achieving success in our schools*. New York: Basic Books.

K–3 school of choice, A. (1990). Grant proposal to Innovation in Education Program (unpublished).

Kidder, T. (1989). *Among schoolchildren*. New York: Avon Books.

Kliebard, H. M. (1972). Metaphorical roots of curriculum design. *Teachers College Record, 73*, 403–404.

Krueger, R. A. (1988). *Focus groups*. Newbury Park, CA: Sage Publications.

Lakoff, G., & Johnson, M. (1980). *Metaphors we live by*. Chicago: The University of Chicago Press.

Lightfoot, S. L. (1983). *The good high school: Portraits of character and culture*. New York: Basic Books.

Little, J. W. (1990). The persistence of privacy: Autonomy and initiative in teachers' professional relations. *Teachers College Record, 91*, 509–536.

Louis, K., & Miles, M. (1990). *Improving the urban high school: What works and why*. New York: Teachers College Press.

Marsh, D. (1988, April). *Key factors associated with the effective implementation and impact of California's educational reform*. Paper presented at the annual meeting of the American Educational Research Association, New Orleans. (ERIC Document Reproduction Service No. ED 303 863)

McNally, D. (1990). *Even eagles need a push*. Eden Prairie, MN: TransForm Press.

Miles, M. B. (1987). *Practical guidelines for school administrators: How to get there*. (Report No. UD 025 918). New York: Center for Policy Research. (ERIC Document Reproduction Service No. ED 288 939)

Mumby, H., & Russell, T. (1990). Metaphor in the study of teachers' professional knowledge. *Theory into Practice, 29*, 116–121.

National Commission on Excellence in Education. (1983). *A nation at risk*. Washington, DC: National Commission on Excellence in Education.

Nias, J. (1989). *Primary teachers talking: A study of teaching as work*. New York: Routledge.

Owen, J. M., Loucks-Horsley, S., & Horsley, D. L. (1991). Three roles of staff development in restructuring schools. *Journal of Staff Development, 12*, 10–14.

Oxford English Dictionary (2nd ed.). (1989). New York: Oxford University Press.

Paprotte, W. (1985). Metaphor and the first words. In W. Paprotte & R. Dirven (Eds.), *The ubiquity of metaphor* (pp. 425–480). Philadelphia: John Benjamins Publishing Company.

Peck, M. S. (1987). *The different drum: Community-making and peace*. New York: Simon and Schuster.

Preskill, H. (in press). Riding the roller coaster of educational change: Evaluation and the learning organization. In P. Jenlink (Ed.), *Systemic change anthology*. Palatine, IL: Skylight Publishing.

Pugh, W. C. (1987). *Ethnography and school improvement research: Analyzing metaphoric language in the interpretation of instructional leadership* (Report No. EA 019 680). Philadelphia: Annual Forum on Ethnography in Education Research. (ERIC Document Reproduction Service No. ED 286 281)

Ravitch, D. (1983). *The troubled crusade: American education, 1945–1980*. New York: Basic Books.

Rich, D. (1988). *MegaSkills: How families help children succeed in school and beyond.* Boston: Houghton Mifflin.

Rich, D. (1991). Parents can teach MegaSkills to their children. *Educational Leadership, 49,* 42.

Rich, J. M., & DeVitis, J. L. (1989). An evaluation of the aims and curriculum proposals in Sizer's *Horace's Compromise.* In C. M. Shea, E. Kahane, & P. Sola (Eds.), *The new servants of power: A critique of the 1980s school reform movement* (pp. 145–151). New York: Greenwood Press.

Rickover, H. G. (1963). *American education, a national failure: The problem of our schools and what we can learn from England.* New York: Dutton.

Ricoeur, P. (1977). *The rule of metaphor: Multi-disciplinary studies of the creation of meaning in language* (R. Czerny, Trans.). Toronto: University of Toronto Press. (Original work published 1975)

Rockefeller Brothers Fund. (1958). *The pursuit of excellence: Education and the future of America* (Panel Report V of the Special Studies Project). Garden City, NY: Doubleday.

Rutter, M., Maughan, B., Mortimore, P., & Ouston, J. (1979). *Fifteen thousand hours: Secondary schools and their effects on children.* Cambridge: Harvard University Press.

Scheffler, I. (1960). *The language of education.* Springfield, IL: Charles C. Thomas.

Scheffler, I. (1979). *Beyond the letter.* Boston: Routledge & Kegan Paul.

Schein, E. (1992). *Organizational culture and leadership* (2nd ed.). San Francisco: Jossey-Bass Publishers.

Senge, P. M. (1990). *The fifth discipline: The art and practice of the learning organization.* New York: Doubleday.

Sergiovanni, T. J. (1989). What really counts in improving schools? In T. J. Sergiovanni & J. H. Moore (Eds.), *Schooling for tomorrow: Directing reforms to issues that count* (pp. 1–7). Boston: Allyn and Bacon.

Sergiovanni, T. J. (1992a). *Moral leadership: Getting to the heart of school improvement.* San Francisco: Jossey-Bass Publishers.

Sergiovanni, T. J. (1992b). Why we should seek substitutes for leadership. *Educational Leadership, 49,* 41–45.

Shakeshaft, C. (1989). *Women in educational administration.* Newbury Park, NY: Sage Publications.

Sirotnik, K. A. (1989). The school as the center of change. In T. J. Sergiovanni & J. H. Moore (Eds.), *Schooling for tomorrow: Directing reforms to issues that count* (pp. 89–113). Boston: Allyn and Bacon.

Smith, W. F., & Andrews, R. L. (1989). *Instructional leadership: How principals make a difference.* Alexandria, VA: Association for Supervision and Curriculum Development.

Stevens, E., & Wood, G. H. (1987). *Justice, ideology, and education.* New York: Random House.

Stockdill, S. H., Duhon-Sells, R. M., Olson, R. A., & Patton, M. Q. (1992). Voices in the design and evaluation of a multicultural education program: A developmental approach. *New Directions for Program Evaluation, 53,* 17-33.

Tager, M. J. (Producer & Director). (1990). *Teamwork* [Video]. Beaverton, OR: Great Performance.

Taylor, F. (1911). *Scientific management.* New York: Harper & Brothers.

Thompson, T. N. (1986). *Analoguing creativity & culture: A method for metaphors* (Report No. CS 505 597). Mt. Pleasant, MI: Central Michigan University, Department of Speech Communication & Dramatic Arts. (ERIC Document Reproduction Service No. ED 282 263)

Tiberius, R. G. (1986). Metaphors underlying the improvement of teaching and learning. *British Journal of Educational Technology, 17,* 144-156.

Tom, A. R. (1984). *Teaching as a moral craft.* New York: Longman.

Tyack, D. B., Kirst, M. W., & Hansot, E. (1980). Educational reform: Retrospect and prospect. *Teachers College Record, 81,* 253-269.

U.S. Department of Education. (1991). *America 2000: An education strategy.* Washington, DC: Author.

Weber, M. (1947). *The theory of social and economic organizations.* New York: The Free Press.

Wolcott, H. F. (1973). *The man in the principal's office: An ethnography.* New York: Holt, Rinehart and Winston.

Index

About the Author

Jean Wincek is a certified presenter of the 4MAT® System and consultant for educational theory and technology for Excel, Inc., in Chicago. She also does adjunct teaching in the Graduate School of Education, Professional Psychology, and Social Work at the University of St. Thomas in St. Paul, Minnesota, and in the School of Graduate and Special Programs at Saint Mary's College of Minnesota in Minneapolis. In both her consulting work and her graduate teaching, Jean team-teaches with her colleague, Colleen O'Malley.

Jean holds a doctorate in educational leadership from the University of St. Thomas in St. Paul, a master's degree in educational administration from the University of Dayton, and a master's degree in theology from the University of Notre Dame, South Bend, Indiana. Her undergraduate degree is in elementary education from the College of St. Catherine, St. Paul, Minnesota.

Prior to studying for her doctorate, Jean served as principal of two K–8 schools for a total of 15 years. She began her educational career as a teacher of seventh- and eighth-grade students. She has written several articles for professional journals and is co-author of the book *Ensuring the Future: The ABC's of Strategic Planning*. Her research interests include school improvement and effective teaching.